The Magic of Bewitched Cookbook

Also by Gina Meyers, The Magic of Bewitched Trivia and More book, The Magic of Bewitched Trivia book.

THE MAGIC OF BEWITCHED COOKBOOK

Clients, Cookery and Cocktails

Gina Meyers

iUniverse, Inc.
New York Lincoln Shanghai

The Magic of Bewitched Cookbook
Clients, Cookery and Cocktails

Copyright © 2007 by Gina Marie Meyers

All rights reserved. No part of this book may be used or reproduced by any means, graphic, electronic, or mechanical, including photocopying, recording, taping or by any information storage retrieval system without the written permission of the publisher except in the case of brief quotations embodied in critical articles and reviews.

iUniverse books may be ordered through booksellers or by contacting:

iUniverse
2021 Pine Lake Road, Suite 100
Lincoln, NE 68512
www.iuniverse.com
1-800-Authors (1-800-288-4677)

Because of the dynamic nature of the Internet, any Web addresses or links contained in this book may have changed since publication and may no longer be valid.

The views expressed in this work are solely those of the author and do not necessarily reflect the views of the publisher, and the publisher hereby disclaims any responsibility for them.

Unless otherwise noted, all photos courtesy of the Gina and David Lawrence Meyers, and Mark Simpson collections.

ISBN: 978-0-595-47760-9 (pbk)
ISBN: 978-0-595-60021-2 (ebk)

Printed in the United States of America

To Fictional Characters in a Reality-Based World! Specific thanks to all the *Bewitched* writers who have turned these figments of their imaginations into supernatural creations!

"The best and most beautiful things cannot be seen or touched. They must be felt with the heart."—Helen Keller

A life fused in negativity is a precious moment lost, an illustrious dream forgotten,
A bright future snuffed out, a life half-lived, a beautiful moment not shared.
What we perceive-we believe, what we believe, we become. Share the joy of cooking, an infectious smile, the beauty of laughter, and The Magic of *Bewitched* Cookbook.–Gina Meyers

The Magic of Bewitched Cookbook
Table of Contents

The *Bewitched* Theme Song Lyrics ix

McMann & Tate Clients xi

The Cast of *Bewitched* xvii

Serena's Saucy Guide to Life xix

Twitch or Treat 1

I've Got A Hunch Lunch, Sandwiches 47

Game Called On Account of Soup 55

Company's Coming Side Salad 58

The Main Dish 62

Breakfast 91

Tales of Toadstools and Barstools
Madison Avenue Mocktails-Non-Alcoholic Beverages 96

Cocktails 104

Increments 110

Larry Tates' Little Black Book of Hangover Remedy Cures 141

Cutting Down On the Fat Content 142

No time for a Supermarket Run 144

Substitutions 145
Weights and Measures 146
Cooking Terms and Translations 148
What's Brewing in the Bewitched Caldron? 149
About the Author 153
Upcoming Books by author Gina Meyers: 157
Index 159

The *Bewitched* Theme Song Lyrics
Words and music by Howard Greenfield and Jack Keller

Bewitched, bewitched, you've got me in your spell.
Bewitched, bewitched, you know your craft so well.
Before I knew what you were doing, I looked in your eyes.
That brand of woo that you've been brew-in' took me by surprise.

You witch, you witch, one thing is for sure—
That stuff you pitch—just hasn't got a cure.
My heart was under lock and key—but somehow it got unhitched.
I never thought my heart could be had.
But now I'm caught and I'm kinda glad to be—
Bewitched Bewitched—witched.

*Note: Lyrics never used for *Bewitched*'s opening or closing credits.

Bewitching Facts:
Larry threatened to fire Darrin in 7 episodes
Larry fired Darrin 19 times
Darrin quit from McMann & Tate twice
Darrin retired once

McMann & Tate Clients

Show	Account	Accounts Client
3	Barker Baby Food	Rex Barker
5	Caldwell Soup	Phillip Caldwell
7	Halloween Candy	Mr. Brinkman
8	_____	Mr. Austen
11	Jasmine Perfume (Miss Jasmine Campaign)	_____
18	Margaret Marshall Cosmetics	_____
20	Woolfe Brothers Dept. Store	_____
21	Jewel of the East (jewelry)	Mr. Pickering
23	Slegershamer's Dairy	_____
30	Feather Touch Typewriters	_____
35	Perfect Pizza Parlors	Linton Baldwin
36	Shelley's Shoes	_____
38	Stanwyck Soap	Mr. Martin
41	E Z Open Flush Door	Mr. Foster
42	_____	Howard Norton
43	(Party Favors)	Jack Rogers
44	Mother Jenny's Jam	Charles Barlow
45	Jarvis Accout; Slater; Murphy Supermarket	_____
46	Toy Ship Models	Mr. Harding
49	Harper's Honey	_____
50	Hotchkiss Appliance Co.	Ed Hotchkiss

52	Kingsley Potato Chips	
53	_____	H.J. Simpson
58	Hockestedder Toy Co.	
59	_____	Randolph Turgeon
60	Aubert of Paris	
	J.T. Glendon	
62	Naisley's Baby Food	
63	Westchester Consolidated Mills James Robinson	
64	Detergent	J.K. Kabaker
65	_____	Osgood Rightmire
66	Robbins Baby Food Co.	
67	Robbins Baby Food Co.	
68	Stern Chemical Co.	Sanford Stern
71	United Cosmetics	Tony Devlin
73	Waterhouse Thumbtack Co.	
75	Robbins Truck Transmissions	Mark Robbins
82	Wright Pens	
83	Macelroy Shoes	
85	_____	Randolph Parkinson, Jr.
86	_____	Max Cosgrove
87	Franklin Electronics	Bernie Franklin
89	Super Soapy Soap	Tom Scranton
92	Solow Toy Company	
93	Sheldrake Sausage	
94	Morton Milk	C.L. Morton
95	Ganzer Garage Doors	
96	Tropical Bathing Suits	
97	_____	Ed Pennybaker
98	Cunningham Perfume	
100	_____	Mr. Morgan
101	Warbell Dresses	Jay&Terry Warbell
102	Baldwin Blankets	Horace Baldwin
	Mayor Rocklin	Frank Eastwood

104	Madame Maruska Lipstick	_____
105	_____ clients unnamed	
106	Saunders Soups	_____
107	Hornbeck Pharmaceutical	_____
108	Rohrbach Steel Company	_____
109	_____	Bob Chase
110	Chef Romani Foods	_____
112	Bigelow Tires	_____
113	Carter Bros. Industrial Products (Anti-Smog Device)	_____
114	Baxter Sporting Goods	Joe Baxter
117	Springer Pet Foods	Alvin Springer
120	Gregson Home Appliances	_____
121	_____	Mr. Grayson
122	Chappell Baby Foods	Roy Chappell
123	Mortimer Instant Soups	Jesse Mortimer
124	Mint Brite Toothpaste	J.P. Pritchfield
125	Autumn Flame Perfume	Bo Callahan
126	Webley Foods	J.P. Sommers
127	Prune Valley Retirement Village	JonathanBrodhurst Leroy Wendell
128	Giddings Tractors	_____
129	Abigail Adams Cosmetics	Mr. Blumberg
132	_____	Dwight Sharpe
134	Baker Foods	Edgar Baker
136	Mishimoto TV Sets	Kensu Mishimoto
138	Omega National Bank	R.H. Markham
139	Hercules Tractors	Charles Gilbert
	Slocum Soup	OJ Slocum
	Angel Coffee	_____
146	Hascomb Drug Company	Whitney Hascomb
147	Zoom Detergent	H.L. Bradley

148	Barton Industries (Tinker Bell Diaper Division)	_____
149	E Z Way Rent A Car/ Sav-Most Markets/ Mossler Enterprises	Harlan Mossler
152	_____	Mr. Stewart
153	Adrienne Sebastian Cosmetic Products	_____
155	Vino Vanita	Clio Vanita
157	"The Fuzzy Doll" Hanley's Department Store	Jim Hanley Mr. Henderson
158	Dufee's Dog Food	Oscar Durfee
159	Campbell Sporting Goods	Waldo R. Campbell
160	Struthers Account	_____
162	Brawn Colonge	Evelyn Tucker
164	_____	J. Earl Rockeford
170	Bueno/aka Zap	Raul Garcia
172	Hampton Motors	_____
173	Top Tiger Cologne	Evelyn Charday
174	(A detergent account)	Mr. Paxton
175	Berkley Baby Food	_____
177	Bartenbach Beauty Products (Dental Cream, Hair Tonic, Wart Remover)	_____
178	_____	Alvin J. Sylvester
179	Illinois Meat Packers	_____
180	Bliss Pharmaceutical	Silas Bliss Sr. & Jr.
181	Bliss Pharmaceuticals	Silas Bliss Sr. & Jr.
183	Shotwell Pharmaceuticals	_____
185	Tanaka Electronics (Division of Tanaka Enterprises)	_____
187	Multiple Industries	H.B. Summers
189	_____	Mr. Nickerson
190	Top Pop	_____

191	Braddock Sporting Goods	Bob Braddock
192	Breeze Shampo	_____
194	Harrison Industries	John J. Harrison
195	A housing Development	_____
196	Dinsdale Soups	George Dinsdale
197	Barber Peaches	_____
199	Happy Heart Greeting Card	Augustus Sunshine
200	_____	George Meiklejohn
201	Gotham Industries	_____
202	_____	Ernest Hitchcock
205	Barrows Umbrellas	_____
206	British Imperial Textile Mills	Sir Leslie Bancroft
207	Blakely Account	_____
209	Gibbons Dog Burgers	Charles Gibbons
210	Beau Geste Toiletries	Jennings Booker
211	Bigelow Industries	J.J. Langley
212	Harmon Savings and Loan	_____
214	Bobbins Candy Bonbons/ Bobbins Buttery Bonbons	Bernard Bobbins
216	The Reducealator	Mr. Ferber
218	Rockfield Furniture	Lionel Rockfield
219	Berkley Hair Tonic	Roland Berkley
220	Colonel Brigham's Spareribs	Colonel Brigham
222	Cushman Cosmetics	_____
223	Patterson Account	_____
	Bradwell Account	_____
	Cushman's Restaurant	_____
224	Mother Flanagan's Irish Stew	Sean Flanagan
226	_____	Client in Chicago
227	Mount Rocky Mutual	Harold Jameson
232	Count Bracini's Olive Oil	_____
233	House of Baldoni	Ernesto Baldoni
234	Europa Tours	Henri Sagan

235	Regal Silverware	_____
236	Silverton Toy Company	Lester Silverton
237	Benson's Chili Con Carne	_____
239	Monticello Carpets	Mr. Cushman
240	Tom Cat Tractors Inc.	Mr. Burkeholder
241	_____	Mr. Spengler
243	_____	Elliott Norton
244	Prescott Shoes	Wilbur Prescott
245	Woolcott Towers	Harrison Woolcott
250	Whirlaway Washing Machines	Hector Jamison
252	Benson Sleep-Ezy Mattress	_____
253	Ah Fong's Restaurant	Mr. Fong
254	Cora May Sportswear	Cora May Franklin

J. Edward McKinley was a client on *Bewitched* the most times, with 9 episodes to his credits. Jack Collins and Charles Lane both appeared 7 times. Parley Baer was shown as a client 6 times. Tying for appearing 4 times includes actors' Irwin Charone, John Fiedler, Arthur Julian, Arch Johnson, and Herb Voland. Larry D. Mann was shown 3 times. Edward Andrews, John Gallaudet, George Ives, Nancy Kovack, Oliver McGowan, Cliff Norton, Mala Powers, and Dan Tobin all were on twice.

Trivia Tidbit:

Actress Sara Seegar was a client's wife in seven different episodes.

The Cast of *Bewitched*

ROLE	PLAYED BY
Samantha Stephens	Elizabeth Montgomery (254 shows)
Serena	Elizabeth Montgomery (24 shows)
Darrin Stephens #1 (1964–1969)	Dick York (156 shows)
Darrin Stephens #2 (1969–1972)	Dick Sargent (84)
Endora	Agnes Moorehead (147)
Larry Tate	David White (166 shows)
Louise Tate #1 (1964–1966)	Irene Vernon (13)
Louise Tate #2 (1966–1972)	(Imogene) Kasey Rogers (33)
Gladys Kravitz #1 (1964–1966)	Alice Pearce (28) [d. 3/66]
Gladys Kravitz #2 (1966–1972)	Sandra Gould (29)
Abner Kravitz	George Tobias (54)
Maurice	Maurice Evans (12)
Uncle Arthur (1965–1972)	Paul Lynde (10)
Doctor Bombay	Bernard Fox (18 shows)
Aunt Clara (1964–1968)	Marion Lorne (28 shows)
Tabitha Stephens (1966–1972)	Erin & Diane Murphy (100)
Frank Stephens #1 (1964–1967; 1971)	Robert F. Simon (6)
Frank Stephens #2 (1967–1970)	Roy Roberts (7)
Phyllis Stephens	Mabel Albertson (19)
Esmeralda (1969–1972)	Alice Ghostley (15)
Adam Stephens (1971–1972)	David & Greg Lawrence (17)

OCCASIONAL ROLES

Below is a listing of characters that were occasionally seen on *Bewitched*.

CHARACTERS	PLAYED BY
Aunt Enchantra	Estelle Winwood
Cousin Edgar	Arte Johnson
Cousin Henry	Steve Franken
Cousin Helen	Louise Glenn
Sidney Kravitz	Ricky Powell
Harriet Kravitz	Mary Grace Canfield
Jon Tate	Mitchell Silberman
Aunt Hagatha	Ysabel MacLosky (4 episodes)
	Reta Shaw (4 episode)
The Apothecary	Bernie Kopell
Betty, the secretary	Marcia Wallace
	Samantha Scott
	Jean Blake
The drunk at the bar	Dick Wilson (16 episodes)
Howard McMann	Leon Ames
	Gilbert Roland
Margaret McMann	Louise Sorel

Serena's Saucy Guide to Life

Everyone gets bored of the same old routine, even free-spirited, single Serena. In Episode #161, "Marriage Witches' Style", Serena decides she wants to settle down and marry a mortal, just like her cousin Samantha. Serena consults with a mortal computer dating service who matches her with Mr. Franklyn Blodgett. As it turns out, Mr. Blodgett is a warlock, tired of his warlock ways, seeking mortal love also. After a whirlwind romance and seeming compatibility, Serena and Franklyn both decide to reveal their true identities. After a few minutes of amusement and laughter over having found one another, Franklyn makes the mistake of critiquing Serena's style of magic and the two go their separate way. But not before Serena settles the score of uppity Mr. Blogett and put him in his place by zapping up a giant-sized champagne glass. As Serena would say, "au revoir and good riddance!" Preferring the other side of the cosmos. Below are some simple recipes for a saucy guide to life, brought to you by Serena.

Serena's Saucy Guide to Life

> Rich craft is just as good as witchcraft, any day.
> Flying is the only way to travel.
> Mortal men are always Tall, Dark, and Nothing! (Unless they are rich, bien sur!)
> Mortal Rock Singers are way cool, except when they refuse to sing your song, and have to be coaxed.
> The ever-changing beauty mark is in vogue, and keeps one mysterious, any questions???
> Brunettes have more fun!!!
> Children are nice to visit, but I wouldn't want any of my own.
> Just remember, you only think the grass is greener on Morning Glory Circle, the closer you get, you'll discover that there are weeds.
> Short and sassy is always sexy. (In skirts and hairstyles, that is.)
> Nothing is for sure, eat dessert first.
> Cher, Madonna, Serena, Enough Said? Good!!!
> Doing relatives a favor is a real drag.
> Don't date married warlocks.
> Sing, even if you're off key.

Food fights are fun, especially with friends. (Watch out for that flying, frozen banana!)

Moonthatch Inn. (Sometimes we end up in places we shouldn't be. Take the road less traveled, just make sure you have a map, and that the bed is out of service)

Monkey see, monkey do. (Don't monkey around with my cousin's hubby.)

Claim it, own it, be it.

If you are ever stuffy, take an allergy pill.

Peace, love, and Rock N' Roll.

My Theme Song: "She's A Super Freak"

When you don't know what to do, pop out. (Not to be confused with a wardrobe malfunction.)

Cooking and cleaning is for the birds!

Never look for your ideal mate through a dating service.

There is always Paris and Plastic surgery.

"Samantha Stephen's is hem-deep in ticky-tacky, a clean-scrubbed, suburban Everywoman, with her caldron hooked to the rotisserie." (Look Magazine, January 1965)

Imagine this. You are invited to a dinner party with all of your favorite *Bewitched* Characters. Samantha, of course will be there, charming, elegant, talkative. Darrin will be pitching his latest advertising campaign. Larry will be bending over backwards to impress the client. Louise will be watching Larry's alcohol intake carefully. Endora will be plotting on how to ruin Darrin's client dinner. Gladys will be peeping through the slats in the Venetian blinds looking for a tasty morsel of outrageous gossip to share with Abner. Abner will be practicing his sardonic reply to his wife's crazy nonsensical ravings about the Stephens. Arthur will be practicing his latest absurd practical jokes and doing comical jabs, "Hiya Sammy". Maurice will be reciting a Shakespearian Monologue. Tabitha will be in her room occupying herself by making her stuffed animals dance a pas de deux. Esmeralda will be in the kitchen trying to make a soufflé, but instead makes a real life person materialize. Dr. Bombay will be unavailable as he is busy with one of his "trained" nurses. Aunt Clara will be stumbling on her words. Serena will be flirty, fun, and fascinating. "Weelll", as Samantha would say, you are in luck. Dinner is served!

Here's the dish. Circa 1995, I had been shopping around my *Bewitched* Cookbook, hoping some big publisher would bite. I received a phone call from an editor at a large publishing house who told me that Kasey Rogers (the beloved Louise Tate #2) and companion Mark Woods were in the process of publishing a *Bewitched* cookbook also. Thus, the hopes of having my cookbook in print were temporarily dashed, and it was placed on the back burner. However, things really started brewing in 2004, when I published my first book, *The Magic of Bewitched Trivia and More*. In June of 2005, while on the Warner Brothers' lot for a tour of the *Bewitched* house facade, there I met Kasey and Mark. They were very sweet and cordial, but it was a warm day so they excused themselves early, as Ms. Rogers was recovering from a recent hospital stay. What happened next was truly a moment of fate. An hour or so later, my husband David and I decided to go out to lunch before heading back home. As fate would have it, Kasey and Mark chose the same restaurant. Ms. Rogers agreed to come on a book signing to Glendale, California. She encouraged me to continue with The *Bewitched* Cookbook. So here is The Magic of Bewitched Cookbook, ten plus years in the making, luckily none of the dishes will take that long to create! Bon Appetite. Just remember, cooking is a lost art, rediscovered, but Samantha, a witch, was willing to hang up her broom to learn how to cook the mortal way. Why? Because she knew that the way to Darrin's heart was through her efforts in trying to cook, not what she actually created.

Author Gina Meyers with her graphic designer husband David Meyers

Lauren and Lucas Meyers proudly displaying Bewitched Memorabilia.

Twitch or Treat

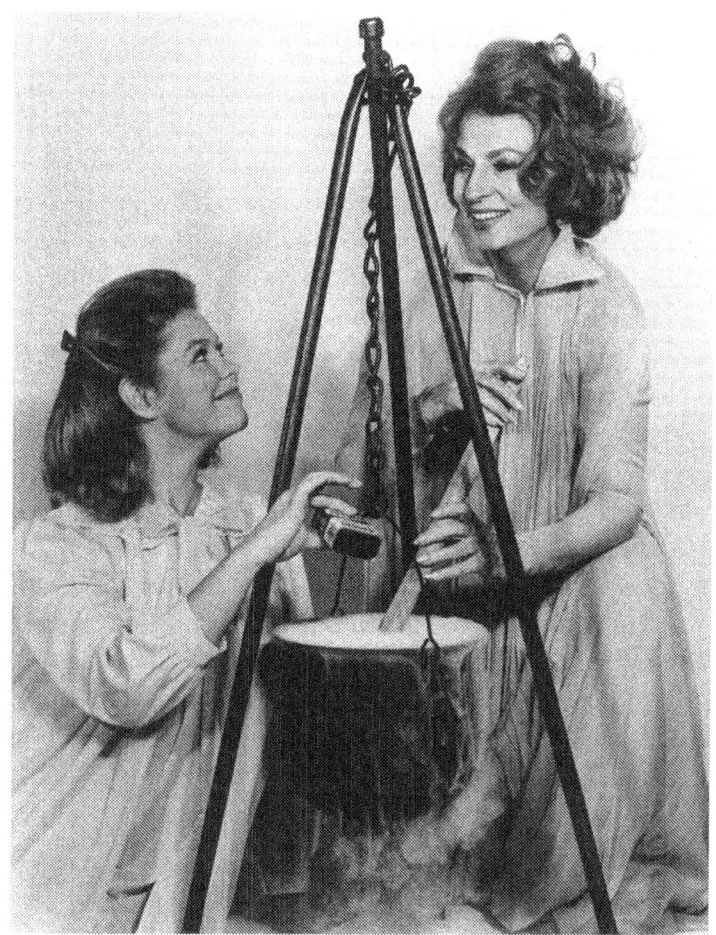

Samantha and Endora posing by a caldron. Gina Meyers collection

Double, Double toil and
Trouble, cookies guaranteed
To get you home on the double.

"Life is uncertain, eat dessert first!"—Gina Meyers

Many Bewitched Episodes dealt with the everyday tasks of a typical suburban house witch. Samantha had to learn literally from scratch how to garden, sew, cook, make a drink, and clean the house.

In our attempts to be the perfect wife and house witch we sometimes run into snafus along the way. Samantha Stephens demonstrated more than just a housewife with a secret. We are all housewives with secrets and hidden talents. She showed us how to handle uncomfortable situations with grace and style. In Episode #3, "It Shouldn't Happen To A Dog", Samantha is trying to create an elegant dinner party and instead Mr. Barker who lives up to his name, wants Samantha's undivided attention. She turns him into a dog, as he is ready to attack her with unwanted affection only later to be misunderstood by her husband Darrin. Darrin later sees Mr. Barker for the low life dog that he is, and puts him in his place, by punching him out. Mr. Barker later admits, "Hey I have a problem."

Samantha Stephens represents an ideal for young girls even today. Like Lucille Ball, Elizabeth Montgomery exuded her own special brand of magic and comic timing.

"Darrin, I bet she's good at typing, the checkbook, cooking, and cleaning, all the things that little old me can't do."—Sheila Sommers, Darrin's former girlfriend.

In Episode #233, "*Bewitched*, Bothered and Baldoni", Endora makes the statue of Venus come to life which causes trouble for Darrin. All of the men, Darrin, Larry, and Mr. Baldoni, McMann & Tate's Italian client, become infatuated with Venus, thinking she is an extraordinary woman by the name of Vanessa. What they don't know, is Vanessa really is the Goddess of Love. Darrin is so smitten with Venus, a.k.a. Vanessa, that Darrin brings Vanessa back to the Villa that he and Samantha are renting while on business/vacation in Italy. Darrin insists Samantha give her a job as a maid. Because Vanessa is a flirtatious Goddess, and is really a statue, when Samantha asks her to get dressed, Vanessa gets a little confused about appropriate maid attire.

Samantha: "Vanessa, when I said an apron, I didn't mean just an apron. Now, why don't you be a good girl and go out—backwards?"
Samantha to Darrin: "She may be many things, but inexperienced isn't one of them."

"When I come home, I like a little food and a little relaxation."—Darrin, from "Red Light Green Light".
"I don't want to simmer like a watched pot, I want to get out and boil."—Serena

In Episode #192, "Serena Stops the Show," Serena wants the rock group Boyce and Hart to come sing at the Cosmos Cotillion, an annual dinner dance for witches and warlocks. When Serena approaches the duo about singing her song entitled, "I'll Blow You A Kiss In the Wind", their manager gives her the big kiss-off as they decline her offer. Serena has the last laugh as she makes the once hip group unpopular by casting a spell on the entire teenage public. In the end, they sing Serena's song, and Samantha requests that Serena send, "those howling Hippies back to earth!" (Serena had zapped them out of the Cosmos to a Cotillion party).

In Episode #192, "Serena Stops the Show", Serena goes cloud-hopping with rock duo Tommy Boyce and Bobby Hart to perform her song, I'll Blow You a Kiss in the Wind", at the Cosmos Cotillion. Serena posing with the rock duo Tommy Boyce and Bobby Hart. Mark Simpson collection.

Cosmos Cotillion Cream Cheese Cookies
16 ounce package of cream cheese
¼ cup of margarine
1 package of lemon cake mix
1 egg
1 tsp. of vanilla extract

Directions: Preheat oven to 375 degrees. Mix the margarine, egg, and cream cheese in a bowl until well blended. Add vanilla extract and the cake mix. When mixed, roll the cookie mixture into balls and place on an ungreased cookie sheet. Bake dough for 8 minutes.

Cosmos Cookies
1/2 cup of margarine
3/4 cup of confectioner's sugar (powdered sugar)
1 Tablespoon of vanilla extract
1 1/2 cups of flour
1/8 teaspoon of salt
Food coloring-optional
Chocolate pieces, peanut butter chips, nuts, cherries.

Galaxy Icing (to complement Cosmos Cookies)
Mix together:
1 cup of confectioner's sugar
3 1/2 Tablespoons milk
1 teaspoon of vanilla extract
Food coloring-optional

Directions: Heat oven to 350 degrees. Thoroughly mix together margarine, vanilla, sugar, and three drops of food coloring (any color). Add flour and salt and work until dough can hold together.

Mold dough by Tablespoonfuls around a few chocolate pieces, nuts, or cherries. Place cookie dough on a baking sheet approximately 1 inch apart for 10 minutes or until light brown.

Once the cookies are cool, dip tops of cookies into Galaxy Icing. Decorate cookies with colored sugar, sprinkles, candies, or coconut. Yields 25 cookies.

I'll Blow You A Kiss In The Wind Song
(By, Tommy Boyce and Bobby Hart & Serena)

Whenever you are tonight
I got a feelin' that you look out of sight,
So I'm gonna blow you a kiss in the wind.

And when it reaches your lips your lips my dear,
You're gonna smile and feel me oh so near,
So I'm gonna low you a kiss in the wind.

I've been laying here in my bed
The images of pretty thoughts runnin' through my head
About a guy in my mind I can feel
I can almost touch
Oh, my goodness
I miss you and I want you so much.

Wherever you are tonight
I got a feelin' hat you look out of sight
So I'm gonna blow you a kiss in the wind.
Yeah, I'm gonna blow you a kiss in the wind.

Mocha Kiss Chocolate Chip Cake
1 package of Butter Fudge Cake mix
1 small package of instant vanilla pudding
4 eggs
1 pint of sour cream
¼ cup of chilled strong coffee, such as French or Espresso roast
½ cup of vegetable oil
8 ounces of semi-sweet or milk chocolate chips

Directions: Mix all ingredients in a bowl with an electric mixer. Place batter into a sprayed bunt pan and bake at 350 degrees for forty minutes. Check if the cake is done, by placing a toothpick in the center. If the toothpick comes out clean, the cake is baked and ready to take out of the oven. Cool and serve. Once cooled, generously dust top of cake with powdered sugar.

Dick Sargent as Darrin in Episode #177,
"To Trick or Treat or Not To Trick or Treat."

Halloween Pumpkin Cookies

2 cups of all-purpose flour
1/2 teaspoon of baking powder
1 teaspoon of vanilla extract
1 teaspoon of cinnamon
1/4 cup of butter or margarine, softened
3/4 cup of shortening, such as Crisco brand
1-cup of sugar
1-cup of canned pumpkin
1/2 cup of pecans, chopped
1/2 cup of dates, chopped

Directions: Combine all dry ingredients. Next, combine vanilla extract, butter, shortening, sugar, pumpkin and mix until well-blended. Then add ingredients together, add pecans and chopped dates. Using a Tablespoon, spoon mixture onto a sprayed cookie sheet and bake at 350 degrees for ten minutes.
*Perfect Halloween Holiday treat.

Marshmallow Burns Rice Crispies

In Episode #6, "Little Pitchers Have Big Fears", Samantha helps a young boy, named Marshall Burns, to try out for the baseball team. Marshall's mother is terribly overprotective and it has left the young boy feeling inferior. Gladys Kravitz says his nickname is Marshmallow.

3 Tablespoons of Margarine
1 package of regular marshmallows
6 cups of rice crispy cereal

Directions: Melt margarine and marshmallows in a bowl in the microwave for one minute. Remove from the microwave and add the rice crispy cereal and mix with a wooden spoon. Place mixture in a 9x9 inch sprayed pan and mold the rice crisipies with a piece of waxed paper. May add colored candies, such as mnm's to the Rice Crispies for added flavor and color.

**Jimmy Mathers as Marshall Burns from "Little Pitchers Have Big Fears".
Gina Meyers Collection**

"Gee Wiz Mr. Stephens."—Marshall Burns

Marshall Burns' nickname is:
   Smokey the Bear
   Burnt Burns
   Marshmallow Burns

What sport does Marshall desperately want to play?
   Baseball
   Football
   Soccer

What fruit does Marshall's mother say he is allergic to?
   Apples
   Strawberries
   Cantaloupes

True/False
Samantha helps Marshall in his quest to play sports.

Marshall Burns is played by Jerry Mathers of Leave It to Beaver Fame.

Answers: Marshmallow Burns, baseball, strawberries, true, false (Jimmy Mathers)

Pumpkin Fudge
3 cups sugar
¾ cups margarine
½ cup of evaporated milk
½ cup of pumpkin pie filling
1 package of white chocolate chips
1 jar of marshmallow cream
1 tsp. of vanilla extract
1 Tbs. of pumpkin pie spice

Directions: stir together the sugar, margarine, evaporated milk and pumpkin pie filling in a sauce pan. Bring to a boil, stirring constantly. Remove from heat, and add in the chocolate chips until they are melted. Mix the remaining ingredients until well blended. Pour into a greased 9x9 inch pan. Cool. Cut into squares. May wrap in colored saran wrap. Fudge keeps best when wrapped in waxed paper or individually in saran wrap.

Pumpkin Chocolate Chip Muffins
2 large eggs
½ cup of low fat milk
½ tsp. of vanilla extract
½ cup of light brown sugar
1 cup solid packed pumpkin
4 Tbs. margarine, melted
¾ cup of heavy cream
½ cup of semi-sweet chocolate chips
½ tsp. cinnamon
¼ tsp. salt
¼ tsp. nutmeg

Directions: Mix all ingredients by hand in a bowl or with an electric mixer on low speed. Place batter mixture into muffin tins and bake at 375 degrees for 15 to 18 minutes.

"Don't shave the fuzz off your peaches, let Barber do it."—Barber Peach Jingle

Barber Peach Crisp
5 cups of sliced peaches
½ cup of rolled oats (such as Quaker Oats, a main sponsor of *Bewitched*)
½ cup of all-purpose flour
½ cup of light or dark brown sugar
¼ teaspoon of nutmeg, ginger, and/or cinnamon
¼ cup melted margarine
Optional: ¼ cup of coconut or nuts

Directions: Preheat oven to 375 degrees. Melt margarine in the microwave or on the stovetop. Place peaches in a glass or round baking dish. Next, in a mixing bowl, combine oats, brown sugar, flour, and spices. Pour dry mixture over the peaches (the peaches have been placed in either a round or rectangular glass baking dish). Pour the melted margarine over the peaches as well as sprinkling the dry mixture. Bake in a 375 degree oven for 30 minutes, or until fruit is tender and topping is a golden color. Can serve with ice cream or whipped cream as a topping to this warm, yummy dessert.

Frog's Eye Salad

In Episode #106, "Nobody but a Frog Knows How to Live", Fergus F. Finglehoff was once a frog who has now been transformed into a man. Samantha tries to help Fergus change back into a frog.
(Was a favorite recipe of the late Linda Wells Hill, stepmother to the author)

½ lb. package Acinidi Pepe (small round ball pasta)
1 egg
½ cup of granulated Sugar
1–15oz. can crushed pineapple tidbits (drain pineapple and reserve juice)
1—20oz. can fruit cocktail
1—cup cool whip
1/3 cup of pineapple juice (can use from crushed pineapple juice reserve)
1 Tbs. of flour
¼ tsp. salt

Directions: Cook Acinidi Pepe according to package directions. Beat egg till foaming in a pan. Then stir in sugar, flour, salt, reserved pineapple liquid, and pineapple juice. Cook over low heat and stir until bubbling. Combine mixture with drained pasta. Cover mixture tightly and allow chilling in the refrigerator overnight. Next day, stir in fruit cocktail and cool whip.

What is Fergus's girlfriends' name?
  Febbie
  Freddie
  Felicia

What type of soup will Saunders' launch as Number 59?
    Frog
    Turtle
    Moose

What does Fergus call Samantha?
    Lady
    Girlie
    Sammy

Answers: Febbie, Turtle, Girlie

Makenna Meyers posing by the popcorn hands that she helped make prior to a Halloween party. Circa 1998. Photo courtesy of David and Gina Meyers Collection.

Gina Meyers helping at a class party, October 2004.
Photo courtesy of the David and Gina Meyers collection.

Popcorn Hands
Popped popcorn
Clear latex gloves
Candy corn
Black or orange curly ribbon

Directions: place candy corn in each of the five finger spaces, to resemble fingernails. Next place popcorn inside the latex glove. If using microwavable popcorn, make sure the popcorn has cooled. Works best with kettle corn or plain, non buttered popcorn. Close with a piece of curly ribbon.

Monkey Bread

In Episode #155, "Serena Strikes Again", Serena turns Darrin's sexy Italian client Clio Vanita into a monkey, when she makes a play for Darrin behind Samantha's back. In this two-part episode, Clio the monkey escapes and Samantha goes looking for the missing chimp. Once they find her, Serena turns her back into a human and Samantha announces Darrin's slogan. "Don't monkey around with anything but the best, drink Vino Vanita."
*Kid Friendly; children can easily help create this bread.

1 loaf of thawed Bridgeford bread, rolled into balls (frozen bread such as Bridgeford brand)
½ cup (1 stick) of melted butter or margarine
½ cup of sugar and cinnamon mixture

Directions: Roll out balls of thawed bread, and dip them into melted butter. Once dipped in the melted butter, then roll them in sugar-cinnamon mixture and layer the sugar cinnamon balls into a sprayed bunt pan. Bake at 350 degrees for 25 minutes, or until done.

Which actress played the role of Clio Vanita?
    Kasey Rogers
    Kit Smythe
    Nancy Kovack

This actress guest starred on *Bewitched* in another role. Name her character?
    Daphne Harper
    Sheila Sommers
    Pleasure O'Riley

Answers: Nancy Kovack, Sheila Sommers

I Want to be Butterfly Buns

In Episode #151, "I Don't Want to Be a Toad, I Want to Be a Butterfly", Grandmother Phyllis enrolls Tabitha in the Delightful Day Nursery School. Tabitha meets fellow classmate

Amy who wants to be a butterfly. Tabitha turns Amy into a butterfly, and Samantha chases Amy up a tree, a skyscraper, and then Tabitha transforms Amy back into a little girl. Their teacher Mrs. Burch believes she needs a vacation after witnessing magic.
*Kid Friendly Recipe

1 tube of refrigerated cinnamon rolls with icing (usually 8 in a package)
8 maraschino cherries

Directions: Separate rolls and cut in half. Place on a greased baking sheet with the cinnamon side up and curve the edges to form wings. Cut the cherries into six wedges, place three on each wing. Bake according to package directions. Cool cinnamon buns. Lastly, with the icing, place in a plastic bag, or pastry bag, cut a small hole in the corner of the plastic bag and pipe icing out to outline the wings. Makes eight butterflies.

Gladys Kravitz Sugar Cookies

"I came over for a snoop, uh, a scoop of sugar. I hope I'm not disturbing you."
—Gladys Kravitz, world's nosiest neighbor asking to borrow a cup of sugar from Samantha.

"Abner, I'm going over to the Stephens to borrow a cup of sugar."—Gladys Kravitz

(The reason why she was borrowing so much sugar from Samantha)
1 cup of butter
¼ cup of milk
1 teaspoon of vanilla extract
4 cups of flour
2 eggs
1 ½ cups sugar
1 teaspoon of baking soda

Directions: Cut butter into flour. Combine sugar, eggs, and vanilla. Mix all ingredients together. Knead and roll out onto a floured surface. Press down sugar cookie dough with a rolling pin. Next, trim with cookie cutters of your choice, such as silly shapes or sizes. Place on a baking sheet. Bake at 350 degrees for 8 to 10 minutes. Yields three dozen.

My Boss the Teddy Bear Cookies

In Episode #49, "My Boss, the Teddy Bear," Darrin thinks Endora has turned Larry into a stuffed teddy bear. There is much confusion as Endora brought back a teddy bear for Larry and Louise's son and Louise too had purchased a bear at the department store. Darrin purchases all the bears at the department store, thinking one of them is his boss.

"Twenty four teddy bears all nodding yes to Harpers Honey."—Darrin's slogan for Harpers Honey.

¾ cup of shortening
½ cup of sugar
½ cup of packed brown sugar
1 egg
1 tsp. of vanilla extract
2 cups of all-purpose flour
1 tsp. salt
½ tsp. baking soda
30 mini milk chocolate kisses
60 mini baking m&m candies
Chocolate frosting or icing
¼ cup of sugar

Directions: Combine in a mixing bowl, shortening and sugars. Beat in egg and vanilla extract; mix well. In another bowl, with a wooden spoon, mix dry ingredients. Mix wet and dry ingredients together. Reserve about ½ cup of the cookie dough for the teddy bears' ears. Shape the remaining dough into 1 inch balls and roll into the extra sugar. Flatten the balls and place on a lightly greased cookie sheet. Use the reserved dough to make smaller balls and roll into the extra sugar. Flatten two small balls onto the cookie sheet to make the bears' ears. Bake at 350 degrees for 10–12 minutes, or until the cookies are light brown in color. Once the cookies have cooled, place a chocolate kiss in the center of the cookie for the nose and 2 m&m candies for the eyes. Use a dab of frosting on the chocolate kiss and m&m's to make then stick onto the teddy bear cookie.

Name Larry and Louise Tate's son.
   Teddy
   Jonathan
   David

Name the actress who played Louise Tate #2.
   Irene Vernon
   Elizabeth Montgomery
   Kasey Rogers

Answers: Jonathan, Kasey Rogers

Trivia Tidbit:

Irene Vernon was the original Louise Tate. She left to pursue a career in Real Estate.

Trivia Tidbit:

Kasey Rogers, Louise Tate the second, was an actress and later became an author of cookbooks, entertaining, and craft books.

Mother Jenny's Jam Cookies

In Episode #44, "The Very Informal Dress", Darrin invites Clara and Samantha to go with him to a client dinner party. Clara conjures up party clothes for Darrin and Samantha to wear to the cocktail party, except there is a problem. The clothes start to disappear. When the three arrive at the party, there is no parking. Clara zaps away a fire hydrant, and it later reappears, causing Darrin to get a ticket and also causing a ruckus with Darrin's lack of proper attire. His clothes disappear and he is left in a tee shirt and underwear. While at the cocktail party, Aunt Clara tries Mr. Barlow's concoction and doesn't like the taste. These cookies are yummy and are guaranteed to vanish in an instant!

Mother Jenny's Jam Cookies
2 ½ cups of all-purpose flour
½ teaspoon of baking powder
1 cup margarine or butter, softened

1 egg
1 cup of white sugar
2 teaspoons of vanilla extract
1 cup of your favorite flavor of fruit jam
Makes 4 dozen cookies

Directions: Preheat the oven to 300 degrees. In a bowl, combine flour and baking powder. Mix well and set aside. Next, in a medium sized bowl, cream butter/margarine and sugar, egg, and vanilla extract. Beat with an electric mixer until smooth. Then add the flour mixture and blend on low speed until combined. Roll the dough into 1 inch balls and place on a baking sheet, approximately 1 inch apart. With your thumb, press down the center of the dough balls and shape the ball to form a circle in the middle of the ball. Place a small amount of jam in the center of the dough ball, about ½ of a teaspoon of jam. Bake 20 minutes in a 300 degree oven until golden brown.

"I better go get Mrs. Stephens cookie cutters?"—Gladys
"What's your hurry, are you planning to start baking tonight?" said sarcastically by Abner
"Can you think of anything more exciting to do? Besides, never put off until tomorrow."—Gladys
"What you don't have to do at all."—Abner (Gladys hurriedly walks away from the Stephens Front door in a huff, back to her home.)

Endora summons Serena to take Samantha's place in an attempt to break up Samantha's Marriage.

Double Double Toil and Trouble Cookie Bars

In Episode #145, "It's So Nice to Have A Spouse Around the House", Samantha goes to a Witches Council meeting and Serena shows up pretending to be Samantha. Darrin mistakenly takes Serena on a second honeymoon to the Moonthatch Inn, and Serena tries to fend off Darrin's advances. He later learns it wasn't his wife on the second honeymoon, and Darrin figures out his error once back at home.

1/2 cup margarine or butter
1 1/2 cups gram cracker crumbs
1 (14 ounce) can sweetened condensed milk
1 (6 ounce) package of semi-sweet or milk chocolate chips
1 1/3 cup of coconut flakes
1 cup of chopped walnuts

Directions: Preheat the oven to 350 degrees. Melt butter in the microwave and add gram cracker crumbs to the melted butter. Next, in a 13x9 inch baking pan, place gram cracker crumb mixture and press down with a fork, covering the bottom of the pan. Then, pour a can of sweetened condensed milk on top of gram cracker crumb mixture. Then sprinkle the remaining ingredients of chocolate chips, nuts, and coconut flakes and bake for 25 minutes. Once cooled, cut into bite size squares. Creates a delicious concoction of chocolate and coconut. You may add peanut butter chips, or white chocolate chips to the recipe if you desire.

Moonthatch Inn Coconut Lemon Crumb Squares
1 ¾ cups of Graham cracker crumbs
½ cup granulated sugar
¾ cup margarine, melted
¾ cup all-purpose flour
½ cup of coconut

Filling
½ cup of granulated sugar
1 egg
1 cup of lemon juice, plus ¼ tsp. of lemon rind
½ coconut

Directions: Melt the margarine and pour over the first ingredients. Combine in a large bowl and work together until crumbly. Press the mixture into an ungreased 9x9 inch pan and set aside.
Next, place filling ingredients in a pot on low heat, stirring until thickened. Pour filling over bottom layer. Cook for 25 minutes in a 350 degree over. Depending on the size you cut for the squares, makes approximately 30 squares.

Bobbins Buttery Bonbons

In #214, "Mother in-law of the Year", Endora is asked to promote Bobbins Candy Campaign by being the spokesperson for one of their products, Bobbins Buttery Bonbons.

The Bobbins Candy show is called the "Sweetheart Parade", and gets a 37% share. The Henry Mancini song from 1965, "The Sweetheart Tree" played in the background in Episode #214.

Bonbons
1/4 cup melted butter
1 can sweetened condensed milk
1 lb. powdered sugar
1 package coconut
1 package chocolate chips
1/2 cube Parowax

Directions: Combine butter, milk, sugar and coconut. Chill at least 30 minutes. Form into small balls and chill again. Melt chocolate chips and wax over hot water. Dip balls into chocolate mixture quickly and remove with fork. Put on waxed paper to cool. Makes 2 dozen bonbons.

"I'll just hate myself in the morning."—Mrs. Dumont, committee chair after taking a second one of Samantha's secret cookies.

Peanut Butter Pie
1 carton frozen whipped topping (8 ounces)
1 ready made graham cracker crust
½ cup strawberry jelly
1 cup cold milk
1 package instant vanilla pudding mix
½ cup of creamy peanut butter

Directions: Spread 1 cup of the whipped topping over the bottom of the crust. Drop jelly by the tablespoonfuls onto topping. In a bowl, whisk milk and pudding mix until thickened.

Add peanut better; mix well. Then, fold in the leftover whipped topping, spread over the jelly. Allow to harden in the freezer for at least 4 hours. Serves 6–8.

Hot Fudge Sundae

In #248, "Tabitha's First Day at School", Tabitha turns a class bully named Charlton into a frog. When the child's mother, Mrs. Rollnick, discovers that her son is missing, she locates him at the Stephens' house, and Tabitha turns Charlton back into his original form.

"We're gonna stop at the ice cream parlor and get you a great big hot fudge sundae with almonds on top."—Mrs. Rollnick
"And flies?"—Charlton

Hot Fudge Sundae
Vanilla ice cream
Fudge
Blanchard almonds
Assorted candies
Strawberries, blackberries, blueberries
Maraschino Cherries
Whipped Cream

   Directions: Heat fudge in either a saucepan or in the microwave. Place on top of softened ice cream. Top off with almonds and whipped cream (flies are optional).

Chocolate Covered Bananas

In #165, "Samantha's Power Failure", Serena and Uncle Arthur lose their powers when they side with Samantha against the Witches' Council's demand that Samantha dissolve her marriage to Darrin. Serena and Uncle Arthur decide to find out how the other half lives by getting jobs at a local ice cream store making chocolate-covered bananas. The results are messy as Serena and Uncle Arthur end up having a chocolate banana fight at the store. The episode is very reminiscent of Lucy and Ethel in the candy factory in the *I Love Lucy* television series. William Asher actually directed the candy factory episode from *I Love Lucy*.

Chocolate Bananas

4 bananas
8 Popsicle sticks
Magic Shell, any flavor
Wax paper
Toppings: m n m candies, nuts, coconut, chocolate chips.

Directions: Peel and cut bananas in half widthwise. Place Popsicle sticks into each of the 8 banana halves. On a piece of wax paper, place the banana, drizzle with magic shell and add any toppings, if desired. Wrap the banana in the wax paper and place in freezer for 2 hours, or until bananas are frozen. Bananas will be ready for eating and can be kept in freezer for several days.

Aunt Sue's Cake

In Episode #161, "Marriage Witches Style", the Aunt Sue's cake mix jingle is recited.

> *Put your trust in Aunt Sue's Cake Mix*
> *You will find it's not a fake mix*
> *It will make a better batter*
> *And it weighs lighter than fatter.*
>
> *It will make your batter better*
> *And it weighs lighter than a fetter.*

Aunt Sue's Cake Recipe

1 1/4 cups All-purpose Flour
1 cup sugar
1 1/2 teaspoons baking powder
1/2 teaspoon salt
3/4 cup milk
1/3 cup shortening

1 egg
1 teaspoon vanilla extract

    Directions: Heat oven to 350 degrees. Grease and flour a square pan. Put all of the ingredients in a large mixing bowl. Blend for 3 minutes on high speed, while scraping the sides of the bowl. Pour into the floured pan. Bake 35 to 40 minutes. Cool, then eat and serve.

Midnight Chocolate Cake

In #97, "I Remember You Sometimes", Endora puts a spell on Darrin's wristwatch, which gives him total recall on any and all subjects. This causes Samantha to become upset while fixing Darrin breakfast because he brings up useless information that she interprets as malicious and hurtful.

Darrin: "… and remember that enormous chocolate cake you whipped up by witchcraft."

2-1/4 cups flour
1-2/3 cups sugar
2/3 cup cocoa
1-1/4 teaspoons soda
1 teaspoon salt
1/4 teaspoon baking powder
1-1/4 cups water
3/4 cup shortening
2 eggs
1 teaspoon vanilla extract

Directions: Heat oven to 350 degrees. Grease and flour two 9-inches round layer pans. Place all ingredients into a large bowl and blend together with a spoon or with an electric mixer on low speed. Beat 3 minutes on high speed. Take a spatula and scrape the sides and bottom of bowl, make sure all of the ingredients have been mixed well. Pour the batter into the two greased and floured pans.
Bake for 30–35 minutes or until tooth pick inserted in center comes out clean. Cool. Top with Cloud 9 frosting.

Cloud 9 Frosting
1/2 cup sugar
1/4 cup corn syrup
2 Tablespoons water
2 egg whites
1 teaspoon vanilla extract

Directions: Place sugar, syrup and water in a saucepan. Cover the saucepan, and boil over medium heat. As the mixture boils, beat egg whites until stiff. Pour mixture from saucepan slowly into egg whites, beating constantly with electric mixer on medium speed. Add vanilla extract while beating.

"Do you know how to make pineapple upside down cake?"—Phyllis to Samantha
"Oh, no."—Samantha

Pineapple Upside-Down Cake

In #14, "Samantha Meets the Folks", Darrin meets Aunt Clara for the first time. Aunt Clara fixes coq au vin for dinner and pineapple upside-down cake for dessert.

1/4 cup butter or margarine
1/2 cup brown sugar
1 can sliced pineapple, drained
7 maraschino cherries
6 pecan halves
Cake batter-use Aunt Sue's Cake recipe

Directions: Heat oven to 350 degrees. Melt butter and place in a round layer pan, 9x1–1/2 inches. Sprinkle brown sugar evenly over butter. Cut and place pineapple slices at the bottom of the pan and arrange. Place the cherries and the pecans around the pineapple slices. Prepare cake batter. Pour evenly over pineapple. Bake 35 to 45 minutes. Cool and then invert onto a plate.

Frothy Champagne Dip

In "Thars Gold in Them Thar Pills", Samantha says, "Champagne has been known to work wonders." Inside the champagne is a magic formula prescription via Dr. Bombay's caldron to catch a cold, to rid the side effect of a high pitched voice, however, their cold resumes.

3 eggs
¼ cup of sugar
1 Tbs. finely grated orange peel
2/3 cup of whipping cream
2/3 cup of medium dry champagne
Fresh strawberries

Directions: Place eggs, sugar and orange peel in a small bowl. Set bowl over a pan of simmering water and beat until mixture is thick and fluffy. Remove bowl from heat and beat in whipping cream and champagne. Serve dip with fresh strawberries and slices of lemon or vanilla cake.

"Champagne has been known to work wonders."—Samantha

Samantha serves champagne to Darrin, Larry, and two clients to help rid the side effect of:
   a.   A high pitched voice
   b.   Growing Hair
   c.   Common Cold

Dr. Bombay gives Samantha a prescription for:
   a.   antidepressants
   b.   how to catch a cold
   c.   how to make chicken soup

Answers: high pitched voice, how to catch a cold

Prune Cake

"It looks like a king size prune."(in regards to the roast Naomi has just baked)-said by Louise to Naomi, an inept cook who Louise hires from Samantha and Darrin for a formal dinner party she is hosting.

1 cup prunes, pitted and chopped
1 package of active dry yeast
½ cup of warm water
3 cups all purpose flour
1-teaspoon salt
½-teaspoon baking soda
1-teaspoon pepper
2 Tablespoons room temperature butter
¾ cup buttermilk (if you don't have buttermilk on hand, look at the Substitutions guide to make your own version of buttermilk)
½ cup of walnuts (optional)

Directions: Dissolve yeast in ½ cup of warm water. In a separate bowl, stir the dry ingredients of flour, baking soda, salt, and pepper, then make a well in the middle. Next, add the chopped prunes, buttermilk, and room temperature butter. Pour in the yeast mixture. With a wooden spoon and your hands, mix together the ingredients, adding more flour if needed. Take out of the bowl, and knead on a floured wooden surface. Return to the bowl and cover with a clean dish cloth and leave in a draft free environment for about 1 ½ hours, or until the bread has doubled in volume. Place on a greased baking sheet and shaped into a long cylinder shape. Cover again with the dish cloth and leave to rise in a warm area for about 30 minutes. Brush top with milk or egg and bake in a preheated 425 degree oven for 10 to 12 minutes. Lower the heat to 75 degrees and bake for an additional 30 to 35 minutes.

Chocolate Pudding

It is revealed in #163, "Tabitha's Weekend", that Tabitha's favorite dessert is chocolate pudding.

1/3 cup sugar
2 tablespoons cornstarch
1/8 teaspoon salt
2 cups milk
2 egg yolks, slightly beaten
2 tablespoons butter
2 teaspoons vanilla

Directions: Blend sugar, cornstarch and salt in a saucepan (2-quart). Combine milk and egg yolks; gradually stir into sugar mixture. Cook over medium heat, stirring constantly, until it thickens. Boil and stir 1 minute. Remove from heat, stir in butter and vanilla. Serves 4.

Lemon Meringue

(Recipe courtesy of Linda Ferrari, authors mother)
*Darrin's favorite dessert is Lemon Meringue.
"Double, Double, Toil and Trouble," episode #111, had its' share of pie throwing. Darrin and Samantha hit each other with pies. Apparently, the cast had so much fun, they had to dub Elizabeth Montgomery's lines twice, and then decided to leave in the giggles and crack-ups.

Recipe for pie filling
Bring to a boil in saucepan:
1 cup water
3/4 cup sugar
1/4 teaspoon salt
1 teaspoon grated lemon peel

Directions: Add: 5 Tablespoons cornstarch, blended with 1/2 cup cold water. Cook over low heat until thickened (about 5 minutes) stirring constantly. Remove from heat. Add separately, mixing well each time

2 well-beaten egg yolks
1 Tablespoon butter
6 Tablespoons lemon juice
Pour into 8-inch pie shell. Top with meringue.

Meringue

Directions: Add gradually: 4 Tablespoons sugar to 2 egg whites beat until frothy. Continue beating until egg holds its shape and peaks. Fold in 1 Tablespoon of lemon juice. Cover pie and brown in 325 degree oven for 15 minutes.

Butterscotch Bars

Inspired from "Samantha's Da Vinci Dilemma", butterscotch flavored toothpaste.

In Episode #124, Aunt Clara summons Leonardo Da Vinci to paint the Stephens home. Aunt Clara tries to send Mr. Da Vinci back to the past, but is unable. Mr. Da Vinci becomes upset once he learns that his famous Mona Lisa painting will be used to sell toothpaste for one of Darrin's clients advertising campaigns. Samantha creates another campaign with Leonardo's likeness on the package and with flavored tooth paint. In the end, Aunt Clara is able to send Mr. Da Vinci back in time.

1-Cup of all-purpose flour
6-Tablespoons of brown sugar
1/8 teaspoon of salt
½ cup of butter or margarine
6 ounce package (1/2 of a package) of butterscotch chips
1-Tablespoon of Corn syrup
1-Tablespoon of Water
2-Tablespoons of butter or margarine
1/8 teaspoon of salt
2/3 cup of walnuts, chopped (optional)

Directions: In a bowl, stir together flour, brown sugar, salt and margarine or butter. Next, press the crumbled mixture into an ungreased 9x9 inch pan. Bake in a 375 degree oven for 10 minutes. Next, combine the remaining five ingredients into a saucepan on low heat. Melt mixture and then add the walnuts, if desired. Pour the mixture over the first layer and place back into a 375 degree oven for 8 minutes. Once cooled, cut into squares. Makes approximately 25 Butterscotch bars.

Napoleon

In Episode#147, "Samantha's French Pastry", Uncle Arthur ruins Samantha's Angel Food cake and decides to try and replace it with a fancier dessert, a Napoleon Pastry. Instead, the Emperor Napoleon appears. When Larry sees Napoleon, he believes he would be perfect for a TV detergent commercial. Samantha passes off Napoleon as her cousin Henri from Paris. She also convinces Napoleon to mess up during the commercial spot. Uncle Arthur cannot remember the spell, but accidentally Samantha says, "Bats wings and lizard tails," and this makes Napoleon disappear.

During the episode, Samantha tries to explain to Darrin how Napoleon arrived: "When a witch, or a warlock, casts a spell involving an object … the name of which may also be used to identify a human being, the kinetic vibrations run the risk of zonking across the atmospheric continuum, and the ectoplasmic manifestations which might not ordinarily occur happen."

Napoleon
(A favorite of the late Rose Hill)
Chocolate or vanilla pastry cream
Puff pastry
1 cup powdered sugar
2 Tablespoons water
½ ounce semisweet chocolate chips, melted

Directions: Preheat over to 400 degrees. Use a 17 ounce package of frozen puff pastry, let thaw, and then roll out to 12 by 14 inches. Place on a lightly greased cookie sheet and bake according to package directions, then cool. Once the puff pastry has cooled, cut pastry into thirds lengthwise. Mix powdered sugar and water, stir until smooth, until all the lumps of powdered sugar are gone. Pour powdered sugar mixture over one of the pastry strips. With pour chocolate stripes over the glaze and let sit for 30 minutes. With last two pastry strips, spread cream on top. Chill in fridge for one hour until cream is firm. Place all three strips together. Dust with powdered sugar.

*It is easier to purchase a Napoleon at your local pastry shop. Victoria Pastry in San Francisco sells yummy Napoleons.

Wiggle Worm Pie
Foil Cupcake liners
Chocolate cookies
Chocolate pudding
Gummy worm candies

Directions: Crush cookies in a plastic bag until they are crumbs. Next, spoon chocolate pudding into a cupcake tin. On top of the chocolate pudding, layer with cookie crumbs and gummy worms. Hint: Quick and easy recipe. May use store bought chocolate pudding or utilize a small box of instant chocolate pudding.

Creepy Cupcakes
24 baked cupcakes (bake according to package directions)-Chocolate Cake Mix
24 Nutter-butter (name brand) cookies
Chocolate Frosting
Vanilla Frosting
Tube of chocolate decorator's icing.

Directions: frost cupcakes with the chocolate frosting. Ice the entire Nutter-Butter cookie with white frosting and use decorator's icing to draw spooky expression on each ghost cookie. Place cookie in the middle of the cupcake. Makes 24 Creepy Cupcakes.

Spooky Spider Cupcakes, (Creepy, but yummy!)

"I actually think she is kind of interesting, in a creepy sort of way." Samantha talking to Darrin about her feelings concerning Darrin's ex-girlfriend Sheila.

Spooky Spider Cupcakes
1 package of chocolate cake mix
1 package of thin (rope) black licorice

Cup cake liners
Red hot candy

Directions: follow the chocolate cake mix directions and bake cupcakes in cupcake tins. Once cooled, frost with chocolate frosting, and add black licorice for spider legs and place two red hot candies in the center of the cupcake for the eyes.

"I'm a witch!" "A broom riding, caldron stirring, house haunting, card carrying witch!"—Samantha

Ice Cream Witches
(Makes one ice cream witch)
Wacky Ingredients
1 Sugar Cone (witches hat)
Hardening chocolate syrup (like Magic Shell)
Pistachio or mint chocolate chip ice cream
2 candy coated chocolate pieces (witches eyes)
1 piece of candy corn (witches nose)
1 strand of red licorice (witches mouth)

Wacky Tools
Ice cream scoop
A plate

Directions: place a scoop of ice cream on a plate and put a sugar cone on top of the ice cream. Next, on the round ice cream scoop, place the two candy coated chocolate pieces to serve as eyes, the piece of candy corn to serve as the nose, and the red licorice to make the mouth. Drizzle the chocolate syrup over the sugar cone.

Optional: You can sing the song, "I Scream, You Scream, We all Scream for Ice Cream Witches!"

Trivia Tidbit: Shelly Berman, actor who played Mr. Brinkman in Episode #7, "The Witches are out", has fond memories of working with the Bewitched cast in this first Bewitched Halloween episode.

In, "The Witches are out", Darrin is assigned to create a logo for a new Halloween candy, produced by client Mr. Brinkman. Darrin, pitches an old ugly crone as the trademark per his clients request and ends up upsetting Samantha, Aunt Clara, and witch friends Bertha and Mary who view this as a derogatory image of witches. The ladies set out to haunt Mr. Brinkman until he changes his view of witches.

Mr. Brinkman's Halloween Candy
Orange and black peanut MnM candies
Vanilla chocolate chips, 8 oz. package
2 cups pretzel twists
Wax paper

Directions: line a cookie sheet with waxed paper. Melt vanilla chips in microwave. Pour melted chips onto waxed paper and spread with a spatula. Next, add peanut mnm's and pretzel twists. Once cooled, break off into pieces.

Scary, spooky, Ghost Pops. Don't scare your pop with one of these!

Ghost Pops
White chocolate chips
Banana
Mini chocolate morsels
Raisins
Popsicle sticks
Waxed paper

Directions: cut a banana in half widthwise. Place on a piece of waxed paper. Place a Popsicle stick into each of the halves. Microwave white chocolate chip pieces in a microwave safe bowl for approximately three minutes. Once melted, with a spatula, scoop out the melted chocolate and drizzle over the two banana halves. Then, add raisins and mini chocolate morsels for the eyes and nose of the ghost. Wrap in waxed paper and place in the freezer until firm, about two hours.

Light as a Fetter Lemon Pie

(Darrin brainstorming on an ad campaign to install a crosswalk in Morning Glory Circle, from Episode #23, "Red Light, Green Light".)
"Honey, That was delicious, now what's for dessert?"
"You just had it."—Samantha
"That little piece of pie?"—Darrin
(giggling) "I'll get you another piece."—Samantha

Ready Made graham cracker crust
1 (3 ounce) package lemon flavored Jell-O
1 cup boiling water
½ block soft tofu
4 ounces of light whipped topping
1 Tablespoon of fresh lemon juice
1 teaspoon of lemon rind.

Directions: Dissolve the Jell-O in boiling water and cool. Add the tofu and blend with an electric mixer. Fold in the cool whip and add the lemon juice and rind. Pour into graham cracker shell and refrigerate until set. *This is a good substitute for lemon meringue pie if you are watching the calories.

"He's as American as apple pie."—Episode #110, "Business Italian Style," said with an Italian accent by Chef Romani comments directed to Darrin.

Apple Bread

¾ cup of vegetable oil
1 cup brown sugar
2 eggs
1 ½ cups chopped apple
¼ cup chopped walnuts
1 Tbs. lemon zest
1 ½ cups of flour
1 tsp. cinnamon
½ tsp. nutmeg

1 tsp. baking soda
¼ tsp. salt

Directions: Mix all ingredients and pour into a loaf pan. Bake at 350 degrees for 55 minutes, or until toothpick inserted comes out clean.

Raisin Cookies

In #163, "Tabitha's Weekend", Tabitha turns herself into a raisin cookie because she is upset over the adult fighting that is going on. After the incident, Endora and Samantha have a dispute over whether or not Tabitha should be disciplined for turning herself into a raisin cookie.
Endora: "I always tell the truth-as I see it."
Sam: "Mother, you are an incorrigible witch."
Endora: "And you are an insensitive, selfish, mortal marrying child."
Sam: "You don't have to get that huffy about it." (Endora pops out angrily)
Sam: "I guess she does have to get that huffy about it. Oh well … Mom???"

Also in this episode, Endora asks Phyllis about her raisin cookies.
Endora: "They're not by chance from an Alice B. Toklas recipe?"
Phyllis: "They're my recipe."
Endora: "Then I think I'll pass."

1/2 cup shortening (part butter or margarine)
3/4 cup sugar
1 egg
1/2 teaspoon lemon extract
1 3/4 cups all-purpose flour
3/4 teaspoon cream of tartar
3/4 teaspoon baking soda
1/4 teaspoon salt
1 cup raisins

Directions: Heat oven to 400 degrees. Mix thoroughly shortening, sugar, egg, and lemon extract. Blend flour, cream of tartar, baking soda, and salt. Stir into shortening mixture. Mix in raisins. Roll into 1 inch balls. Place about 3 inches apart on a non-greased baking sheet. Flatten with fork dipped in flour. Bake 8 to 10 minutes.

In "Tabitha's Weekend," Esmeralda hexes Tabitha's milk in order to get Tabitha to eat. Samantha accidentally drinks the milk and ends up getting Voracious Ravenousities. Esmeralda's incantation, "As the trumpets sound with a shimmering beat, she who drinks this, will crave to eat."

Trivia Tidbit: In Episode #169, "Samantha's Shopping Spree," Cousin Henry played by Steve Franken, is incorrectly listed in the closing credits as "Uncle Henry."

Oh Cousin Henry Bars

Graham crackers
1 cup brown sugar
½ cup butter
½ cup of milk
1 1/3 cups of graham cracker crumbs
1 cup of chopped walnuts
1 cup of coconut
¼ cup dried cherries.

Directions: Line a 9x9 inch pan with whole graham crackers. In a saucepan, combine sugar, butter, and milk. Bring to a boil, simmer for about 2 minutes. Next, add cracker crumbs, nuts, coconut and cherries, mix well. Pour over the whole graham crackers and allow cooling. Let stand overnight. May add vanilla icing to top. Cut and serve squares.

Endora's Magic Popcorn

In Episode #85, "Oedipus Hex", Endora creates some magic popcorn which causes anyone who eats it to become very relaxed and lazy. Try this spiced up version of Endora's recipe.

8 quarts of plain popped popcorn
1 cup butter or margarine
½ cup light corn syrup
1 package of red-hot candies.

Directions: Place popcorn in a large bowl and set aside. In a saucepan, combine butter, corn syrup and candies, bring to a boil over medium heat stirring constantly. Pour the mixture over the popcorn and mix thoroughly. Place popcorn mixture onto a baking pan and bake at 250 degrees for 50 minutes. To cool, remove from the pan and place on waxed paper.

"Oh, my stars, it is Mother Goose!"
"Oh, my Goose, it is Mother Stars!"

Sam would often exclaim, "Oh my Stars", whenever something went awry.

Samantha "Oh my Stars" Snack
2 7-inch flour tortillas
2 Tablespoons strawberry cream cheese
¼ cup of raisins
¼ cup of dried cranberries
1 cup finely chopped green apples
1 teaspoon sugar and cinnamon combined

Directions: Finely chop apples and place them in a medium sized bowl. Add cranberries, raisins, and sugar cinnamon mixture and stir. Then, fry the tortilla with one tablespoon of margarine in a skillet till crisp. Place tortilla on a paper towel to take off excess margarine and to cool. Once cooled, spread cream cheese and top with apple concoction.

"I'll volunteer, as long as someone lends me some cookie cutters".-Gladys Kravitz

"I came over for a snoop, uh, a scoop of sugar. I hope I'm not disturbing you."
—Gladys Kravitz, world's nosiest neighbor asking to borrow a cup of sugar from Samantha.

Gladys Kravitz Sugar Cookies
(The reason why she was borrowing so much sugar from Samantha)
1 cup butter
¼ cup of milk
1 teaspoon vanilla
4 cups flour
2 eggs
1 ½ cups sugar
1 teaspoon baking soda

Directions: Cut butter into flour. Combine sugar, eggs, vanilla. Mix all ingredients together. Roll out onto a floured surface. Cut with cookie cutters. Place on a baking sheet. Bake at 350 degrees for 8 to 10 minutes. Yields three dozen.

Serena "I Wanna Date" Oatmeal Cookies

1 cup, 2 sticks of unsalted butter, cooled to room temperature
¼ cup of vegetable shortening
1 cup light brown sugar
¾ cup of granulated sugar
2 large eggs
1 teaspoon vanilla extract
2 ½ cups rolled oats
2 cups all purpose flour
½ teaspoon baking soda
½ teaspoon salt
½ teaspoon ground cinnamon
1 cup dried dates, chopped

Directions: Preheat oven to 375 degrees. In a large bowl, beat the butter and shortening until smooth. Next, add the sugars, again, beating mixture until smooth. Add the eggs, one at a time as well as the vanilla, put aside. In a separate bowl, mix all of the dry ingredients, including the cinnamon. Once the dry ingredients have been mixed, combine the wet ingredients and mix until well combined. Then, stir in the dates. Drop the batter by rounded tablespoonfuls 1 ½ inches apart on a cookie sheet. Bake for 12 to 14 minutes.

Biscotti

¾ cup of butter
1-Cup of Sugar
2-eggs
1 ½ teaspoons vanilla extract
2 ½ cups flour
2 teaspoons of ground cinnamon
¾ teaspoon baking powder
½ teaspoon salt
Almond slices

Directions: In a large bowl, mix butter and sugar with an electric mixer, beating in the eggs one at a time. Next, add the vanilla extract and stir in the flour, baking powder, salt, cinnamon, and almonds. Cover the dough in the refrigerator and chill for ten minutes. Once chilled, take out of the refrigerator and divide the dough into two parts, roll into approximately 9 inch logs. Place the logs on a lightly greased cookie sheet, flatten the logs with our hands prior to baking the biscotti cookies. Bake in a 350 degree oven for 30 minutes. Take out of the oven, and cool for five minutes. While dough is still warm, with a sharp long knife, cut the dough in ½ to inch diagonal pieces. On the same cookie sheet, turn diagonal pieces on their sides and bake for an additional 5 minutes in the same (350 degree oven). Makes about 3 dozen cookies.

In Episode #178, "A Bunny for Tabitha", Uncle Arthur does a magic trick and attempts to procure a bunny rabbit for Tabitha, but instead conjures up a Playboy Bunny. Samantha's vegetarian dinner in Bunny's honor includes: carrot ring, carrot pie, spinach soufflé, hearts of lettuce salad, and a string bean sundae (#178).

Orange Candied Carrots
1 pound of carrots, cut into ½ inch slices
¼ cup of margarine, softened, and cubed
¼ cup of jellied cranberry sauce
1 orange peel strip
2 Tbs. of brown sugar
½ tsp. salt

Directions: cook carrots in water in a skillet for 15 to 20 minutes or until crisp and tender. In a blender, combine margarine, cranberry sauce, orange peel, brown sugar and salt. Cover and process until well blended. Drain carrots and drizzle with the cranberry mixture.

I've Got A Hunch Lunch, Sandwiches

"I don't want to be late for my hunch-I mean lunch."—Darrin

"We better have lunch, I'm starved!"—Samantha

"I can whip up something."—Samantha

The original *Bewitched* script contains the following scene, which was later cut from Episode #23, "Red Light, Green Light"

Endora: "I've prepared your dinner, Derwin."
Darrin: "I didn't know you could cook."
Endora: "Oh, yes. Claudius was crazy about my cooking."
Darrin: "Claudius?"
Endora: "The Roman Emperor."
Darrin: "Didn't he die of food poisoning?"
Endora: "Yes, terrible tragedy."

Sandwiches

In #102, "No More Mr. Nice Guy", Endora places a spell on Darrin that makes everyone dislike him. During the episode, Darrin acts overly nice so a client will like him.
Darrin: "I'll run right downstairs and get you a sandwich. What would you like? Ham? Corned beef? How about a club?"
Mr. Baldwin: "Club? Don't tempt me!"

For Episode #186, "Samantha's Lost Weekend". Esmeralda places an eating spell on Tabitha's milk. Samantha drinks the milk by accident and suddenly can't stop eating!

During Samantha's eating binge, Samantha says: "I just thought of something-let's eat dinner, I'm starved".

Sam says to herself, "Samantha, no joking about it, you're a witch with an eating problem." (Later when speaking with Darrin, Sam says: "Be gentle with me Darrin, I've become a foodaholic."

Corned Beef Sandwich
2 slices bread
Softened butter
2 slices cooked corned beef
Prepared mustard

   Directions: Spread bread with butter. Place corned beef in the middle of the two bread slices and add spread mustard on the corned beef.

Club Sandwich
2 slices bread
Butter
2 slices cold chicken
Mayonnaise
2 crisp slices of bacon
2 slices of tomato

   Directions: Toast bread and spread with butter on one slice and mayonnaise on the other piece of bread. Add chicken, tomato, and chicken to the center of the sandwich.

In Episode #232, "Samantha's Not So Leaning Tower of Pisa," Samantha and Esmeralda go down memory lane. It is discovered that Esmeralda's biggest goof is accidentally making the Tower of Pisa lean. While creating a sandwich for her boyfriend, Esmeralda yells out, "One Tower Special, and make it lean!" (In reference to the meat in the sandwich.)

Jack O'Lantern Grilled Cheese Sandwich
White or cheddar cheese sliced
Margarine
White or wheat Bread
Skillet
Pairing knife

Directions: spread margarine on either side of a white or wheat piece of bread. Place cheese in the middle in a skillet on low heat. Brown both sides till cheese is melted. When cooled, use a knife to cut out triangles for eyes and a triangle for a nose. If you wish, you may also make a jack-o'lantern style mouth.

Teddy Bear Picnic

In Episode # 49, "My Boss the Teddy Bear", Darrin thinks Endora has turned his boss Larry into a teddy bear. Larry gives Darrin permission to take some time off work to take Samantha to a "witch" wedding. Endora is grateful to Larry (for allowing Darrin some time off), so she brings Larry a teddy bear for his son Jonathan. Darrin is sure that Endora has transformed Larry into a bear (Darrin is working on the Harper's Honey account) and therefore tries to track Larry-Teddy Bear down. Darrin and Samantha end up in a department store and purchase all of the teddy bears, thinking one is Larry. In the end, it is discovered that Larry wasn't turned into a teddy bear after all.

Ham and Apple Sandwich
½ cup apple butter
2tsp. onion
½ tsp. mustard
Raisin bread, toasted
A slice of ham
Cheese (provolone, Swiss, or Monterey jack)
Red apples, sliced

Directions: toast the raisin bread. Thinly slice the apples, cheese. When the toast is cool, adds mustard and chopped onions to one side of the toast. On the other slice, place the apple butter and apple slices. Lastly, add the ham and cheese to the sandwich.

While visiting Loch Ness, Serena decides to turn her old warlock boyfriend Bruce back into a warlock, after being the Loch Ness monster for centuries. Miffed at Serena, Bruce turns her into a mermaid. Serena: "Haven't you ever seen a mermaid before?" Darrin: "Yes, but only on a can of tuna."

Tuna Sandwich
2–3 servings
2 slices of Sourdough bread, toasted
1 can of water based tuna, drained
¼ cup of mayonnaise
1 sweet pickle, diced
1 celery stalk, finely chopped

Directions: mix ingredients in a bowl and place in between the two pieces of toasted bread. There will be leftover tuna mix, enough to make two more sandwiches.

Clients Over In an Instant Appetizer

"Sometimes I just feel like the devil."—Uncle Arthur

Deviled Eggs
6 hard boiled eggs
¼ cup of mayonnaise
1 teaspoon of mustard
1 teaspoon of red wine vinegar
Paprika to dash

Directions: Hard boil eggs. When cooled, remove shell and cut lengthwise and remove yolks. Place yolks in a bowl and mash, add the mayonnaise, mustard, and vinegar. Once mashed, place yolk mixture in egg white and dash with paprika.

Darrin mentions that Larry loves Samantha's clam dip, but doesn't eat any of it in Episode #200, "Make Love, Not Hate." In Episode #200, Samantha accidentally pours a love potion into the clam dip she plans to serve to Darrin's client. Everyone who eats it falls in love with the first person they set eyes on.

"Where is the clam dip Samantha?"—Dr. Bombay
"Over there."—Samantha
"I may join him, I could do with a swim."—Dr. Bombay

Clam Dip
4 oz cream cheese
1 6.5 oz can minced clams
2 Tablespoon of reserved clam juice
1/4 teaspoon of white pepper
1/2 teaspoon of sherry
1 Tablespoon of chopped parsley
2 Tablespoon of sour cream
1 teaspoon lemon juice
2 cloves pressed garlic
3 drops Worcestershire
Ruffled potato chips
1 teaspoon of finely diced red onion

Directions: Drain the clams, and reserve the liquid. Next, place the clams in a large mixing bowl and add the remaining ingredients. Then, add about 2 Tablespoons of clam juice to taste. Chill and serve with ruffled potato chips.

Larry Tate thinks Darrin needs a vacation after Darrin comes up with this slogan for Kingsley Potato Chips. "Other potato chips may be like chips that pass in the night, but Kingsley Potato chips make you feel like your chip just came in."

Queen of the Witches Crab Cakes
1 Egg
3 Tablespoons of mayonnaise
4 Teaspoons of lemon juice
1/8 teaspoon of red pepper flakes
1 teaspoon dried tarragon
1 Tablespoon of minced green onions
8 ounces of crabmeat
1 Tablespoon of butter
Round crackers, broken up into cracker crumbs

Directions: In a medium bowl, whisk together egg, mayonnaise, lemon juice, red pepper flakes, tarragon, and green onions. Gently stir in crabmeat, and mix in cracker crumbs, adding as much as desired. Next, heat butter in a skillet over medium heat. Form crab patties and place in the skillet and cook until the patties are golden brown. Makes about four crab cakes.

Artichoke Cheese Squares
(Recipe courtesy of Linda Ferrari)
2 jars of marinated artichoke hearts
1 small onion chopped fine.
1 clove of garlic, chopped
4 eggs
¼ cup of bread crumbs
¼ tsp. salt, pepper, oregano.
1/8 tsp. liquid hot pepper
2 cups shredded sharp cheddar cheese
1 teaspoon of parsley, optional

Directions: Mix all ingredients together and transfer into a greased 7x11 glass baking pan. Bake at 325 degrees for thirty minutes.

Apple Cider Cheese Fondue
4 cups of shredded sharp cheddar cheese
1 ½ Tablespoons of cornstarch
1 ¼ cup of apple cider
¼ of a teaspoon of lemon juice
¼ of a teaspoon of salt
1/8 of a teaspoon of cinnamon
1/8 of a teaspoon of nutmeg

Directions: In a medium sized saucepan, on medium heat, warm cider and lemon juice until simmering. Next, toss cheese and cornstarch together and one handful at a time, place into the simmering apple cider mixture, stirring constantly. Stir in remaining spices. Cover over low heat until thickened. Transfer to a fondue pot to keep warm. May dip toasted bread, sliced cooked sausage, or apple slices, in fondue.

In the Bewitched Movie, Jack Wyatt tells the intrusive waitress to check on the other table to see if they are finished with the hummus.

Hummus
(Recipe provided by Rebecca Backdoud)
1 can of Garbanzo beans
2 cloves
Fresh Garlic
Juice of one lemon
2 Tablespoons of Tahini
½ to 1 teaspoon of salt
Olive oil
Paprika
Toasted pine nuts

Directions: in a food processor, chop garlic and salt until minced. Add the garbanzo beans and lemon juice and process until pureed. While scraping sides, add Tahini and process until light and pasty. Make sure that the Garbanzo beans are thoroughly pureed before adding the Tahini. Spread on a plate and drizzle olive oil, sprinkle paprika and pine nuts on top. Serve with slices of pita bread or veggies.

Ants on a Log
Celery stock
Peanut butter, smooth kind
Raisins

Directions: break off a celery stock, wash and dry it. With a knife, or plastic spoon, spread peanut butter onto the celery stock. Top the peanut butter with raisins (black ants) or dried cranberries (red ants).

In Episode #6, "Little Pitchers Have Big Fears", while Samantha tries to explain the game of baseball to Endora. Endora mistakes the word baseball bat for a real live bat. "Yes, I know what a bat is." "Those ugly flying things people always think we're cooking."

Another reference to bats is a conversation between Samantha and Darrin about Serena. "Sshh, Serena may still be hanging around."—Samantha "I'm sure she is, upside down from a rafter in the attic!"—Darrin

Bat Chips
1 large flour tortilla
Cooking spray
Assorted Halloween Cookie cutouts
Salt (optional)

Directions: preheat your broiler. Using Halloween cookie cutters, cut out bat or ghost shapes on the tortilla. Spray cookie sheet with cooking spray and broil until brown. May sprinkle sides with salt.

Many episodes on Bewitched had clients coming over for appetizers and dinner. This cheese rounds recipe is reminiscent of the cheese balls shown.

Cheese Rounds
½ pound of sharp cheddar cheese, grated
1 cup of room temperature butter
2 cups of flour
2 cups of Rice Krispie cereal
A dash of cayenne pepper

Directions: Mix all the ingredients together and shape into small balls. Flatten the balls with a fork. Bake on a greased cookie sheet 1 inch apart at 350 degrees for 15 minutes.

Worms on a Bun
Hot dogs
Hamburger rolls
Ketchup and mustard
*A Halloween recipe for kids or the young at heart.

Directions: cut the hot dogs into thin slices and score the edges. Boil the hotdogs until the slices curl into wiggly worms. Serve worms on a bun. Can add ketchup or mustard to make it extra yucky/yummy!

Game Called On Account of Soup

Food Slogans
"We're nuts about our soup." (Slocan Soup, a McMann & Tate Advertising Account)

Game Called on Account of Soup
Caldwells Leek and Potato Variety

Louise Tate asked maid Naomi to make this consume soup for a client dinner party from Episode #53, Maid To Order.

Parisian Consume
1 can of Campbell's consume soup
1 can of water
3 to 5 button mushrooms, thinly sliced
2 Tablespoons of dry sherry
2 Tablespoons of green onion, thinly sliced.

   Directions: mix soup, water and mushrooms in a saucepan. Bring to a full boil and then add sherry and the onion and serve. Can add parmesan cheese, cooked, cubed chicken, or tortellini to this recipe.

Chicken Soup

In #197, "If the Shoe pinches", a leprechaun who is sent by Endora, invades the Stephens household and creates trouble for Darrin. Samantha brews up a potion to gain control of a leprechaun. As Samantha is reading the recipe out of the spell book, she notices that the recipe calls for chicken soup-a favorite of leprechauns.

Potion
1 cup wolf bane
2 tablespoons of maiden fern, chopped finely
2 eggs from a red eyed kilua bird, beaten
Salt and pepper to taste

Chicken Soup
Zap up 1 chicken
Assorted vegetables

Directions: boil in a pot of water until the chicken and vegetables are tender. Chicken soup is a favorite of leprechauns. Serves 4.

Saunders's Sautéed Turtle Soup

In Episode #106, "Nobody but a Frog Knows How to Live", Saunders Soups' 59th flavor is Sautéed Turtle. The company also makes frozen dinners, chili sauce, and mustard.

Turtle Soup
4 lb. turtle meat
1/2 can tomato puree
1 cup butter
10 cups turtle stock
3 cups chopped white onion
1 cup sherry
1 cup flour
1/2 cup Worcestershire sauce
1 cup parsley
3 hard cooked eggs, chopped finely
1 lemon, thinly sliced

Directions: in a large pot, place turtle meat with 4 quarts of water, 2 bay leaves, 2 cloves of garlic, 6 whole cloves, 2 teaspoons cayenne pepper, and 2 tablespoons of salt. Bring to a boil, cook turtle meat until tender. Once meat is tender, take out of pot and cut into small cubes. Reserve the water from pot as stock. In a skillet, melt butter and sauté onions over medium heat. Stir in flour and cook until browned. Add tomato puree, stock, Worcestershire sauce, and continue cooking for 25 minutes. Add turtle meat, and cook for an additional 15 minutes. Remove from heat, stir in parsley, lemon slices, sherry, and eggs. Makes about 3 quarts of soup.

Taco Soup
1 ½ **pounds of hamburger (browned and drained, salt and pepper to taste as well as onion flakes, about 1 Tbs.)**
1 can corn, not drained
1 can kidney beans, juice as well
1 large can of Mexican or Italian stewed tomatoes
1 can of tomato soup
1 package of taco seasoning mix

Directions: cook the hamburger meat with a little seasoning and drain. In a large pot, add can of corn, kidney beans, stewed tomatoes, can of tomato soup, and 1 can of water as well as the taco seasoning mix. Combine all of the ingredients along with the cooked hamburger meat and simmer for 45 minutes.

Company's Coming Side Salad

"I enjoy taking care of my husband and my child in the everyday mortal way, if I didn't I wouldn't be here."–Samantha

Trivia Tidbit:
In Episode #126, "Snob in the Grass", shows flashbacks to the pilot episode. Nancy Kovack played Darrin's ex-finance in both shows. Sheila refers to Samantha as Sampan, Samovar, Samsarra, Samara, and Stan.

Sheila Sommers Summer Salad
Butter lettuce
Sliced strawberries
Sliced grapes
Sliced apples
4 ounces of vanilla or lemon yogurt
Honey roasted peanuts
1 Tbs. honey
2 Tbs. vinegar
1 Tbs. olive oil
Salt and pepper to taste

Directions: Mix the ingredients together. Place lettuce on a plate and decorate with the fruit and sprinkle with honey roasted nuts.

Broccoli Raisin Salad
1 purple onion, thinly sliced
1 package of fresh broccoli florets
1 cup golden raisins
1 cup mayonnaise
4 bacon slices, cooked and crumbled
2 Tablespoons red wine vinegar

Directions: Stir together ingredients then chill in the refrigerator for two hours.

Esmeralda has plans to go out to dinner and dancing on the planet Jupiter with Ramon Verona. He is the salad chef at the Interplanetary Warlock Club.

"Tabitha, why don't you run upstairs and get ready for dinner."—Samantha

Caesar Salad In episode #173, "Samantha's Caesar Salad", Esmeralda accidentally conjures up Julius Caesar while making a Caesar Salad, and she can't send him back.

Ramon Verona is The Salad chef at the Warlock Club, but in #195, Esmeralda says that he worked at the Interplanetary Playboy Club. In Episode #200, "Make Love, Not Hate", Samantha says, "It's Esmeralda who needs your help. She's had a terrible experience with Ramon Verona." Dr. Bombay responds, "Ate one of his salads, eh?"

2 garlic cloves, crushed
1/2 teaspoon each of salt and pepper
1 tablespoon lemon juice
1 egg, raw or coddled for 1 minute
1/3 cup olive oil
1 head romaine lettuce, washed and torn into bite-sized pieces
1/2 cup grated parmesan cheese
1 cup onion & garlic croutons

Directions: in a large salad bowl, mix garlic, salt, pepper, lemon juice and egg. Add olive oil and mix to combine. Add lettuce and toss. Then add parmesan cheese and onion & garlic croutons. Serves Four.

*Esmeralda has plans to go out to dinner and dancing on the Planet Jupiter with Ramon Verona.

Broccoli Salad
1–2 bunches of broccoli
¾ cup raisins
½ cup red onions, chopped
12 slices of bacon, fried and crumbled

¾ cup of nuts (cashews, peanuts, or sunflower seeds)
Dressing
1 cup of mayonnaise
½ cup of sugar
2 Tbs. red wine vinegar

Directions: cut broccoli into small pieces. Combine with nuts, raisins, onion, and bacon. Mix dressing ingredients and pour over broccoli mixture. Stir together. Chill for 1 to 2 hours.

Cobb Salad
A Full head of lettuce, shredded
1 hard boiled egg
Bacon, cooked and crumbled
Chicken, cooked and cubed
Roma Tomato, chopped finely
Avocado, pitted and cut up
Dressing
1/3 cup Vinegar
1 tsp. salt
¼ tsp. pepper
½ tsp. dry mustard
½ tsp. sugar
1/8 tsp. garlic powder
2/3 cup of salad oil
¼ cup of blue cheese crumbled

Chef's Salad
Head of lettuce, washed, torn, and shredded
Red onion, diced
Green cucumber, sliced
Ham, cubed
Radishes, cut up
Tomatoes, diced
1 hard boiled egg, diced.
*Can also add cubed salami and bologna to your Chief's Salad.

In "Samantha's Better Halves", Endora splits Darrin into two people, one fun loving, the other completely business minded.

Crabby Darrin (my version of Crab Louie)
Small head of Romaine lettuce
1 can of crab meat, or fresh crab meat
1 hard boiled egg, diced
1–2 tomatoes, seeded and chopped
Darrin Dressing
½ cup of mayonnaise
¼ cup of chili sauce
1 tsp. dry onion flakes
1 Tbs. cream or milk
2 Tbs. French dressing
½ tsp. Worcestershire sauce

"Come taste this lobster salad."—Samantha to Darrin

Lobster Salad
Ice berg lettuce, cut
2 tomatoes, cut into wedges
Lobster meat
1 cup of chopped celery
2 hard boiled eggs,
½ cup of mayonnaise
2 tsp. of lemon juice
1 tsp. ketchup
½ tsp. sugar
¼ tsp. of salt

Directions: Combine lobster, celery and eggs in a bowl. Mix the next five dressing ingredients together well, pour over lobster mixture. Top lobster mixture over a bed of lettuce. Place tomato wedges on the side.

The Main Dish

Trivia Tidbit:

Aunt Clara's
In Episode #124, "Samantha's Da Vinci Dilemma", Aunt Clara pops in from the Annual Witches Cookout. There she prepared her favorite dish, Sautéed Pussywillow Almandine.

Name the Italian restaurant that Samantha and Endora try to help publicize.
   A. Luigis
   B. Mario's
   C. Louies

Name Samantha's mother in law?
   A. Phyllis
   B. Alice
   C. Gladys

What does Sam's mother in law often get?
   A. Money
   B. Left out
   C. Sick headaches

answers: B. Mario's; A. Phyllis; C. Sick headaches

Tallerina
In #35, "Eat at Mario's", this is what Endora has to say concerning Italian food.
Endora: "This is the best Italian food I've had this century."
Sam: "You're a great witch, but you're a tough woman."

Tallerina
(Recipe courtesy of Rose Caffaratti)
3 Tablespoons shortening
1 onion, minced
1 lb. ground round
1 cans tomato soup
1 15 oz. can tomato sauce

1 cup cold water
2 Tablespoons salt
2 cups uncooked broad egg noodles
2 cups of whole grain canned corn
1 can ripe pitted olives
1 cup grated cheddar cheese
1 can mushrooms

Directions: melt shortening in a large pot, add onions and cook until brown. Next, add meat and brown; then add tomato soup, tomato sauce, noodles, water, and salt. Cover and cook over low heat for 10 minutes. Remove pot from stove and add corn, mushrooms, and part of the cheddar cheese and mix. Pour entire mixture into a baking dish; cover with remaining cheese and bake at 350 degrees for 50 minutes.

"If you'll excuse me, I'll just pop down to the kitchen and fix myself some scrambled legs—I mean eggs."—Esmeralda
"Does the light really go out when the door closes?"—Darrin asks Esmeralda after she accidentally pops into the refrigerator.

Lemon Soy Chicken Legs
8 whole chicken legs, washed
1 stick of margarine
Juice of one lemon
1 cup of soy sauce.

Directions: Marinate chicken legs for several hours with the lemon juice and soy sauce. Melt margarine over low heat and add the chicken along with the marinade. Fry all sides of the chicken legs till meat is no longer pink in the center.

Esmeralda wants Tabitha to eat better so she places a spell on her milk. Samantha accidentally drinks the milk and ends up becoming addicted to food. While Samantha and Darrin are grocery shopping, Sam's behavior embarrasses Darrin. He ends up asking the clerk, "Where can a find a small rump roast suitable for a bachelor?"

Beef Brisket
1 beef brisket, 2 pounds
1 bottle of BBQ Sauce
1 Tablespoon of garlic powder
3 Tablespoons of paprika
2 teaspoons of brown sugar,
2 teaspoons of onion powder
2 teaspoons of black pepper
2 teaspoons of chili powder

Directions: Rub seasoning on brisket and place in a crock pot; cover with BBQ sauce and cook for 8 hours with lid covered. Makes 4 to 6 servings.

Pot Roast with vegetables.
4–5lbs Pot roast(chuck, round, shoulder or rump roast)
flour
Salt
pepper
1 tsp. sugar
1/2 cup water
1 package Onion Soup mix

Directions: Place tied roast in a deep pot with a lid cover. Dredge roast with flour, salt, pepper and sugar (for browning)
Grease pan lightly. Over high heat, brown roast well on all sides. Will take about 30 minutes. Once dark brown, place rack under the roast. Add 1/2 cup of water and package of onion soup mix. Cover Lower heat and cook very slowly for 2 hrs.
Add: small whole potatoes, tiny onions, small carrots. Coat veggies with the onion soup mix in the pot. continue cooking for another hour or until roast is fork-tender. Don't forget to add a little more water as it cooks, but never have more than 1 inch of liquid at any time. Overall cooking time: 3 to 4 hours serves 8 to 10

Tri Tip

Beef tri-tip, 2 pounds
½ teaspoon of chili powder
½ teaspoon of paprika
½ teaspoon of cumin
¼ teaspoon of garlic powder and onion powder

Directions: Place seasonings on tri tip and refrigerate until ready to grill. On a barbeque grill, roast over medium heat, turning occasionally, about 35 minutes. Carve tri-tip into slices. Makes 4 to 6 servings.

"Well let's see, what would taste good after two hot dogs, popcorn, candy apples, two boxes of peppermint, and popcorn?"—Pretend Samantha, from "Tabitha's Very Own Samantha"

Charlie Harper Winner Wieners

In Episode #99, "Charlie Harper Winner", Darrin met up with his college buddy Charlie Harper. Charlie is rich and successful and doesn't seem to lose. He has all the worldly goods one could desire: a castle, jewelry, a maid, a butler, and expensive clothes. Also Charlie has a snobbish wife by the name of Daphne. Samantha and Darrin teach Charlie and Daphne what is truly valuable.

1 package of hot dogs, sliced into ¼ inch pieces
4 potatoes, peeled and cubed
1 green pepper, sliced
¼ cup of red onion, diced
Vegetable or olive oil

Directions: in a skillet, on medium heat, add 2–3 tablespoons of oil. When warm, add the hot dogs, potatoes, green pepper, and onion. Sautee the ingredients and cook until hot dogs are browned and potatoes are cooked. May add 2–3 tablespoons of water and can reduce heat, if necessary.

Episode Recap

Charlie Harper is an old college pal of Darrin's. Charlie is competitive, handsome, wealthy, and married to a gorgeous snob by the name of Daphne. It seems that everything Charlie Harper does far surpasses Darrin's abilities, or at least Daphne Harper seems to think so. In order to prove to the Harpers' that Darrin is a success, Samantha zaps up a mink coat. This infuriates Darrin because his pride is hurt, he wants to give Samantha material possessions, but cannot afford them. In the end, Samantha teaches Daphne and Charlie a valuable lesson, that material possessions are worthless if you lose the only thing that has any meaning, love.

Trivia Tidbit:

In Gladys' kitchen, in Episode #152, "Weep No More My Willow", there is a wall ornament that resembles a mermaid with a shell border.

Endora's Instant Mashed Potatoes
4 cups chopped white potatoes
¼ cup low-fat milk
Minced garlic
2 Tbs. cream cheese or grated cheddar cheese
½ tsp. tsp. salt
1/8 tsp. pepper
1 can of black beans, drained

Directions: Cut and peel potatoes and place in a saucepan with water. Bring to a boil, and reduce the heat to low. Cook for 20 minutes, or until soft. Once the potatoes are cooked, drain the water and add milk, garlic, cream cheese, salt and pepper. Mash the ingredients with an electric mixer. Once the lumps are out, place potatoes in a pastry bag and squeeze the mashed potatoes onto a lightly buttered cookie sheet. Squeeze in such a way as to resemble ghosts, then place two black beans for eyes. Bake for 5 minutes in a preheated 350 degree oven.

Connecticut Chipotle Mashed Potatoes
3 pounds of potatoes, peeled and cut into 1 ½ inch pieces
¾ cup of milk
1 can (7 ounces) of chipotle pepper
Salt and pepper to taste

Directions: Cut and peel potatoes and place in a large stockpot and cover with water, bringing to a boil. Cook potatoes until tender, then drain. Add milk and chipotle sauce to potatoes and mash. Season with salt and pepper. Makes 6 to 8 servings.

Home-Model Witch

Look Magazine January 26, 1965
"Samantha is hem-deep in ticky tacky, a clean-scrubbed, suburban Everywoman, with her caldron hooked to the rotisserie."

Trivia Tidbits:

In Episode #107, "Thars Gold in Them Thar Pills", Darrin catches a cold and Endora calls in Dr. Bombay who prescribes a pill that cures the common cold. He takes the pills to work and gives one to Larry and a client, who also have colds. Larry excitedly wants to market Bombay's pills, but that is prior to the side effects showing up. The first effect is the pitch of ones voice gets higher. However, the other effect is that it grows hair, a plus to a balding client.

Darrin Stephens was Irish.
Leprechauns are little make believe fairies from Ireland. They are the little old men who are shoemakers for the fairies. They usually stand about two-feet tall. Treasure hunters can find a leprechaun by listening for the shoemaker's hammer. Legend has it that if you catch one you can force him into telling you where his gold is hidden.

In Episode #63, "The Leprechaun", this is the first St. Patrick's Day episode. Brian O'Brian comes to reclaim his pot of gold, which is hidden in a fireplace somewhere in the United States.
Corned Beef and Cabbage is mentioned as Darrin's favorite meal according to Episode #164, "Battle of Burning Oak. (For a simpler recipe, see Easy Corned Beef and Cabbage).

Serena is from Babylon, though she has jokingly told the Stephens' neighbors that she is from the cabbage patch.

Corned Beef and Cabbage
4 pounds of corned beef
1 tsp. oil
2 celery stocks, chopped
1 onion, diced
2 cloves of garlic, minced
2 Tbs. of dried thyme
¼ cup of whiskey
1 tsp. black pepper
2 bay leaves
1 cabbage, cut into wedges
2 Tbs. honey mustard
1 tsp. parsley

Directions: Place all ingredients, except cabbage into a crock pot. Add water if needed. Cook for 7 to 10 hours, or until meat is fully cooked. On the stove top, place a pot with water and cabbage wedges. Cook until cabbage is wilted. Serve hot on a platter along with the corned beef.

"I forgot to defrost the roast, so it is Mother Flanagan to the rescue."—Samantha

Irish stew

In #224,"Out of the Mouths of Babes", Sam sings a jingle as a suggestion for one of Darrin's clients, Mother Flanagan's Irish stew. It is also mentioned in #159, "Samantha, the Sculptress", that one of Darrin's favorite dishes is Irish stew.

Mother Flanagan's Jingle:
If it's for Irish stew you're carin'
You don't have to go to Erin
Ask for Mother Flanagan
And you'll buy can and can again

Irish stew Recipe (Not a Mother Flanagan Recipe)
2 1/2 cups water
1 1/2 pounds cooked lamb, diced
1 teaspoon salt
1/4 teaspoon pepper
2 small onions, sliced
1 turnip, diced
2 medium sized carrots, diced
1 celery stalk, diced
2 cups cubed potatoes

Directions: Place enough water to cover meat in a pot; add onions, turnip, carrots, celery, and potatoes and cook 35 to 40 minutes. Thicken liquid with flour if necessary and serve stew with dumplings.

Dumplings
2 cups sifted flour
1 1/4 teaspoons baking powder
3/4 teaspoon salt
1 Tablespoon butter
2/3 cup of milk

Directions: Sift dry ingredients together. Cut in butter. Add milk to make soft dough. Roll 1/2 inch thick on a floured board. Cut into squares, and drop in hot oil, cook 20 minutes. Makes 10 dumplings.

"Boy something sells good".–Herbie, a boy that Darrin befriends on the basketball court.
"Well, I'm sure your parents will have a nice dinner waiting for you."
Nah, on Saturdays we usually have roast duck, or Cornish hens, or lobster or something dumb like that.

Crepes Suzette

In #116, "Out of Sync, Out of Mind", Samantha makes Crepes Suzette for lunch.

Crepes
1 cup sifted flour
1/2 teaspoon salt
1 tablespoon sugar
3 eggs, well beaten
2 cups milk
2 Tablespoons melted butter
1 Tablespoon cognac
Orangerie sauce:
2 oranges
10 lumps sugar
1/2 cup softened sweet butter
1 teaspoon lemon juice
1/4 cup Grand Marnier
1/4 cup cognac
Crepes (3 crepes per person)

Directions: Sift together flour, salt and 1 Tablespoon sugar into mixing bowl. Combine eggs, milk, melted butter and 1 Tablespoon cognac. Stir in flour mixture. Allow batter to stand 1 hour to improve flavor and texture. Heat a 6-inch crepe pan or skillet and brush the bottom of the pan with melted butter. For each crepe, pour in 2 tablespoons batter. (Spread batter evenly over bottom of pan) Cook, turning once, until nicely browned. Fold crepes into quarters and keep warm.

Wash and dry oranges. Rub sugar lumps over the skin of the orange and then crush lumps into dish. Squeeze juice from oranges into dish. Add butter and lemon juice; cook, stirring constantly, until butter and sugar has melted. Add Grand Marnier and cognac; ignite and quickly pour over crepes.

In Episode #138, "The No Harm Charm", it is mentioned that one of Darrin's favorite dishes is Beef Stew.

Also in #138, "The No Harm Charm", Uncle Arthur first appears in a stewpot. He says, "I'm a stew away." Then he throws a pocket watch in the stew and says that it could use a pinch of thyme, and that it is a watched pot.

Trivia Tidbit

In real life, Dick York expressed that he felt that Samantha should have said to Darrin, "Lay off, or I'll zap you one!"

Trivia Tidbit:
In Episode #10, "Just One Happy Family", Endora is hiding inside the refrigerator from Maurice. She is sitting on a stick of Albain Butter. Dick Albain was the special effects expert on *Bewitched*.

Beef Stew

In episode #246, "Samantha on Thin Ice", Samantha gets annoyed when Endora over-seasons the stew she is cooking.
Samantha: "Mother you may be the salt of the earth, but I wish you wouldn't do that. (Referring to Endora popping a salt shaker and it pouring into Sam's stew) I can season my stew without your help."
Endora: "Well, I was just trying to make things easier. No point in working yourself into a stew."

Beef Stew
4 Tablespoons oil
1 cup Burgundy wine
1 clove garlic, crushed
1 (10 oz.) can beef consommé
2 large onions, sliced
1 (10 oz.) package frozen artichoke hearts
1 Tablespoons butter
1 1/2 teaspoons salt
1/4 teaspoon pepper
18 fresh mushrooms, halved
2 1/2 lb. stew beef
1/2 teaspoon dill weed

Directions: brown beef in oil; add onions, garlic, salt, and pepper. In a pot, place beef mixture as well as dill weed, wine and consommé. Cover tightly and simmer for 1 1/2 hours or until tender. Sauté artichokes and mushrooms in butter and add to meat; simmer an additional 20 minutes. Remove from heat. Top with biscuits and brush biscuits with butter and sprinkle with parmesan cheese.

Lasagna
(Recipe from Victoria Avakian)
1 container, 15 ounces of ricotta cheese
1 egg
1 package, 8 ounces of shredded mozzarella cheese, and 1/3 cup parmesan cheese
1 jar, 28 ounces of Spaghetti Sauce
1 can of tomato sauce, 8 ounces
½ of a 16 ounce box of uncooked lasagna noodles.
Optional: 1 box of frozen chopped spinach, 1 cup of sliced mushrooms, or 1 cup shredded zucchini
Spices to season with: basil, oregano, garlic, parsley, and fenugreek.

Directions: Preheat oven to 350 degrees. Combine ricotta cheese, egg, and parmesan-mozzarella cheese combination as well as the seasonings in a bowl, mix well. Next, spray the bottom of a 9x13 inch pan and place part of the cooked lasagna noodles. Once the noodles are in the pan, start layering with the ricotta mixture, spaghetti sauce, tomato sauce, and remaining noodles. (May add optional ingredients at this time as well). Cover with aluminum foil and bake for 75 minutes in a 350 degree oven. Allow to cool 10 to 15 minutes before serving.

Easy Corned Beef and Cabbage

Another one of Darrin's favorite dinner dishes is Corned Beef and Cabbage which is revealed in #164, "The Battle of Burning Oak".

Easy Corned Beef and Cabbage
4 pounds corned beef
1 large head of cabbage
Oil and vinegar

Directions: Cover meat with cold water and simmer for 3 hours. Add cut cabbage, and cook until tender. Season with oil and vinegar. Serves 8. Can also place the corned beef into a crock-pot and slow cook for 6 hours.

Phyllis' Hollandaise Sauce (Samantha's mother-in-law))
In episode #154, "Samantha's Super Maid," Phyllis questions Samantha.
Phyllis: "Have you mastered Hollandaise sauce yet, Samantha?"
Sam: "I'm afraid not. That recipe you gave me always seems to curdle."

Hollandaise Sauce
1/2 cup butter
2 egg yolks, well beaten
1/4 teaspoon salt
Dash cayenne
1 Tablespoon lemon juice

Directions: melt butter. Add egg yolks gradually to butter mixture, stirring constantly. Place on double boiler and cook over hot water until thickened, stirring constantly. As soon as mixture is thickened, remove from heat and add seasonings and lemon juice. Makes 1 cup. If sauce should separate, beat in 2 Tablespoons of boiling water, drop by drop.
*Hopefully this recipe won't curdle.

Trivia Tidbit:

Aunt Clara and Samantha read from a Cookbook entitled: Sukiyaki, The Art of Japanese Cooking and Hospitality.

In Episode #136, "A Majority of Two", Samantha and Aunt Clara prepare an authentic Japanese dinner for one of Darrin's clients.

Oriental Style Fried Rice
2 Tbs. vegetable oil
1 tsp. salt
1 onion, finely diced
2 eggs, beaten
1 celery stalk, finely chopped
1 cup frozen peas and carrots

1 cup bean sprouts
6 cups cooked white rice
3 Tbs. soy sauce
2 scallions, green onions (the green part), sliced

Directions: cook rice according to package directions. Heat oil in a large non-stick frying pan or wok. Add salt and onion, stirring until tender. Add celery and then stir in eggs and keep cooking till eggs are done. Then, add the frozen peas and carrots and cover and simmer for five minutes, over low heat. Remove the lid and add the rice, scallions and soy sauce.

Festive Rice
1 cup chopped sweet pepper, green and red. If you can find a yellow or orange pepper, they have a tendency to be sweeter tasting.
½ cup chopped onion
2 medium jalapeno peppers, seeded and finely chopped. Or can purchase canned jalapenos, already chopped, 2 Tablespoons.
1 Tablespoon vegetable oil
2 Roma tomatoes, diced
3–4 sprigs of fresh cilantro
¼ teaspoon of salt
2 cups of cooked brown or white rice
1–15 ounce can of garbanzo beans, drained
1 cup shredded Monterey Jack cheese.

Enchilada

In Episode #170, "Samantha and Darrin in Mexico City", working with a Mexican client to introduce his product "Bueno" to the American market, Darrin looks forward to a trip to Mexico City with Samantha. Larry argues that the client will feel slighted unless they meet with the top man, and Larry goes to Mexico instead. Samantha is annoyed at Larry's behavior and says to Larry: "Send us an enchilada or something." Later in the episode, Larry summons Darrin and Sam to Mexico City to salvage the account which he has messed up.

Bewitching fact: Episode #170, Samantha and Darrin in Mexico City" is Dick York's last *Bewitched* appearance.

Cheese Enchiladas
1/4 cup chopped onion
1 tablespoon butter
2 cups Monterey jack cheese, shredded
1 pound white Cheddar cheese, shredded
2 tablespoons chopped olives
2 tablespoons chopped jalapeno chilies
1 teaspoon salt
12 corn tortillas

Directions: cook onion in butter until tender in a frying pan. In a separate skillet, fry tortillas in oil until soft, but not crisp-drain. Add cheeses, olives, chilies, and seasonings to the tortillas and fold in half. Place in a greased shallow baking dish and bake at 350 degree for 20 minutes, or until cheese has melted. Add Enchilada Sauce to taste.

In Episode #92, "Ho Ho The Clown", Gladys wants Darrin to get her on the Build Your Castle television show so she can win a refrigerator and a rotisserie.

"Samantha's Magic Mirror"
Episode #226
Sam: "I cook by mortal methods."
Ferdy: "Oh, really? Isn't that kinda messy?"

Spare Ribs

In #220, "This Little Piggie", Endora turns Darrin into a pig because she says he's being pigheaded. During the episode, Darrin's client Colonel Brigham who specializes in spare ribs shows up at the Stephens house. Samantha and Darrin think quickly on their feet, sing a jingle and convince Larry and the client that Darrin is dressed like a pig for the new Colonel Brigham's Spare Ribs ad campaign and slogan.

Below is the Colonel Brigham's Spare Ribs jingle sung by Samantha and Darrin. Darrin recites the squeal, squeal part because Endora has not yet transformed him from his pig state.

Colonel Brigham's Spare Ribs jingle
Colonel Brigham's Ribs are best
Ee i ee i o
They're sweet and tender, that's no jest
Ee i ee i o
With a (squeal, squeal) here
And a (squeal, squeal) there
Here a (squeal) there a (squeal)
Everywhere a (squeal, squeal)
Buy a bucket of Ribs today
Ee i ee i o

Colonel Brigham's Sweet-Sour Spareribs
1/2 cup pineapple juice
1/2 cup Karo syrup
1 teaspoon salt
2 Tablespoons soy sauce
3 pounds of spareribs, cut into serving pieces

Directions: combine pineapple juice, Karo syrup, salt, and soy sauce in a large bowl. Add spareribs and marinate about 45 minutes. Place ribs in a roasting pan. Roast about 1–1/2 hours at 350 degrees. Brush ribs with marinade. Makes 4 servings.

Trivia Tidbits

Client Clio Vanita's monkey only eats spaghetti.
Client Phillip Caldwell sells Caldwell Soups.

"Sweet pizza of revenge"—quote said by Darrin

In Episode #35 "Eat at Mario's", Samantha and Endora find out that their favorite Italian restaurant, Mario's, is closing due to competition from pizza chains. To help boost sales and public awareness, Samantha and Endora decide to advertise on Mario's behalf. Samantha creates a full page ad in the newspaper. Endora also adds her own touch by plugging Mario's during a television program. All of this advertising for Mario's infuriates Mr. Baldwin, a client of McMann and Tate. Mr. Baldwin owns a line of successful pizza chains and wants the same treatment that witch-assisted Mario is receiving. Once Samantha realizes that Darrin could be fired, she asks Endora for assistance to save the potentially jeopardized Baldwin account. Endora then decides to do her own mass advertising on behalf of Perfect Pizza Parlors. In the park, Mr. Baldwin hears a child whine, "If I can't have Perfect Pizza, I don't want anything!" He also sees a dog anxious to try Perfect Pizza. In the end, the account is saved.

Create Your Own Perfect Pizza
English Muffins
Pizza or spaghetti sauce
Mozzarella cheese
Pineapple chunks
Pepperoni
Black olives
Green pepper
Fresh sliced mushrooms

Directions: slice all of the ingredients into bite sized pieces. Grate the mozzarella cheese and place the pizza or spaghetti sauce on an English muffin. After the sauce is on the muffin, add cheese and your favorite toppings. Place the pizza on a cookie sheet and bake at 350 degrees for 6 minutes or until cheese is melted.

Client Mr. Baldwin owns Perfect Pizza Parlors. His Perfect Pizza comes in 21 varieties. What is Mr. Baldwins' first name?
- a. Clinton
- b. Linton
- c. Winston

What town does Mr. Baldwin say he is from?
- a. Fresno
- b. Modesto
- c. Sacramento

Answers: 1. B. Linton; 2. B. Modesto

Pasta with Broccoli and Artichokes
1 pound bow tie pasta
Broccoli halved
Pepperoni, cut into 1 inch slivers
Marinated artichoke hearts, diced
½ cup of sun dried tomatoes
3 green onions, chopped
1 Tbs. red-wine vinegar
¼ tsp. salt
¼ tsp. pepper
¼ cup of parmesan cheese

Directions: in a pot, cook pasta in lightly salted water for 10 minutes, or until bow ties pasta is tender. Add broccoli to boiling water in the last five minutes of cooking, then drain. Add the cooked pasta to a bowl and add the other ingredients, and toss. Serve hot or cold. Parmesan cheese as a topping is optional.

Darrin's snobbish side in (#164, "The Battle of Burning Oak") prefers chateaubriand, Lobster Newburg, and caviar.

Lobster Newburg
4 frozen South African rock lobster tails, 4 ounces each

3 tablespoons butter
1/2 cup sherry
1/8 teaspoon paprika
1/8 teaspoon dry mustard
1 can condense cream of mushroom soup
1/3 cup light cream
Salt, pepper to taste

Directions: dice lobster meat and sauté in hot butter until it turns white, then add sherry. Simmer gently until the liquid is reduced to half its original volume and the lobster is tender. Add paprika, mustard, soup, and cream. Simmer 5 minutes. Salt and pepper to taste.

Samantha thinking out loud in Episode #86, "Sam's Spooky Chair", "Boston. Beans. Tea party. Nothing."

Boston Baked Beans
2 Cups of Navy Beans
½ pound of cooked bacon
1 onion, finely diced
3 Tablespoons of molasses
2 teaspoons of salt
¼ teaspoon black pepper, ground
¼ teaspoon dry mustard
½ cup of ketchup
1 Tablespoon of Worcestershire sauce
¼ cup of brown sugar

Directions: Soak the navy beans overnight in cold water. The next day, use the same water and simmer the beans in a pot for about 1 hour. Arrange beans in a bean pot or a casserole dish, placing a portion of the beans in the bottom of the dish and then layering them with bacon and onion. Next, in a saucepan, combine the molasses, salt and pepper, ketchup, mustard, brown sugar and Worcestershire sauce. Mix and bring the mixture to a boil and then pour over the beans. Cover the casserole dish and bake for three hours in a 325 degree oven. Cook until beans are tender, add more liquid if needed.

"Apparently, Darrin is allergic to chicken cacciatore."—Samantha

Chicken Cacciatore
1–3 pound whole fryer chicken, cut into pieces and washed
½ cup of oil
Garlic salt to taste
2 Tablespoons of chopped parsley
1 clove of garlic
Pinch of thyme
2 leaves of sage
1 sprig of rosemary
1 small can of Italian stewed tomatoes, chopped
1 small can of tomato sauce
1 can of button mushroom, drain

Directions: Cut and wash chicken pieces. In a deep frying pan, place oil and cut pieces of chicken, sprinkle with garlic salt and cook until chicken has browned. Once the chicken has browned, add the herbs and spices as well as the tomato sauce, chopped tomatoes, and mushrooms. Cook on high heat for thirty minutes.

In Episode #14, Samantha Meet the Folks", Darrin meets his parents at the airport. This is the conversation that transpires between Darrin and his mother Phyllis. "Have you been eating the right foods Darrin?"—Phyllis Stephens "Honestly mom, I feel great!"—Darrin "Never mind, I'll fatten you up with some good old fashioned home cooking."—Phyllis Stephens "Meet my wife, the diplomat."—Frank Stephens "Sam's a pretty good cook too mom."—Darrin "Oh, I'm sure she is dear." "I just thought I'd give her a few tips though."—Darrin

In Episode #171, "Sam and the Beanstalk", Tabitha switches places with Jack (from the Jack and the Beanstalk storybook) because she is upset over the expected arrival of her baby brother. Tabitha believes that her parents prefer boys over girls. Samantha follows her into the storybook to convince her to come home.

Samantha and the Beanstalk Green Bean Casserole
3/4 cup milk
1/8 tsp. Pepper
10 3/4 ounce cream of mushroom soup
2 (9 oz.) packages of frozen green beans, cut and thawed
3 oz. of French fried onions

Directions: in a casserole, mix all ingredients, except the French fried onions. Bake in 350 degree oven for 30 minutes and then place French fried onions on top and bake for an additional 5 minutes (or until onions are brown.)

"I'm sure you try to cook the things Darrin likes, but perhaps I better give you a recipe for some of his favorite dishes."—Phyllis Stephens, Darrin's mother speaking to Samantha.

From "Red Light Green Light".
"Didn't I teach you to never play with sharp objects?"—Endora
"I'm not playing mother, I'm working".-Samantha
Samantha is having a hard time carving the ham, and Endora uses her powers and instantly creates slices of meat.
"It is simpler that way."—Endora
"Not in a long run, you know Darrin doesn't like me doing that sort of thing."—Samantha
"I'm surprised he doesn't insist you tear it up with your fangs."—Endora

Darrin explains to Samantha what Larry's idea behind business dinners are all about. "All part of Larry's selling concept to wine, dine and sign."—Darrin

Apricot Baked Ham
½ fully cooked ham with bone 5 to 7 pounds
20 whole cloves
½ cup apricot preserves
3 Tbs. dry mustard
½ cup packed light brown sugar

Directions: score the surface of the ham with shallow diamond-shaped cuts. Insert the cloves into the cuts. Combine the preserves and mustard, spread over the ham. Pat brown sugar over the apricot mixture. Place the ham on a rack in a roasting pan and bake at 325 degrees for 20 minutes per pound. 10 to 14 servings. Meat thermometer should read 140 degrees.

"Does a turkey laugh at an axe?" Samantha from Episode #227

Coq au Vin (From Episode#159, "Samantha the Sculptress")
2 chicken breasts, split
Salt and pepper to taste
1/3 cup butter
1 ½ cups sliced fresh mushrooms
¼ cup white Burgundy wine

**2 Tablespoons of orange juice
1 teaspoon grated orange rind
1 10 ½ ounce cream of chicken soup**

   Directions: remove skin and bones from chicken breasts, and wash in water. Pat dry. Sprinkle chicken with salt and pepper. Heat butter in a skillet and brown chicken on both sides. Add mushrooms and sauté mushrooms. Add remaining ingredients and simmer until chicken is cooked, about twenty minutes. Serve with white rice.
(Courtesy of Linda Ferrari)

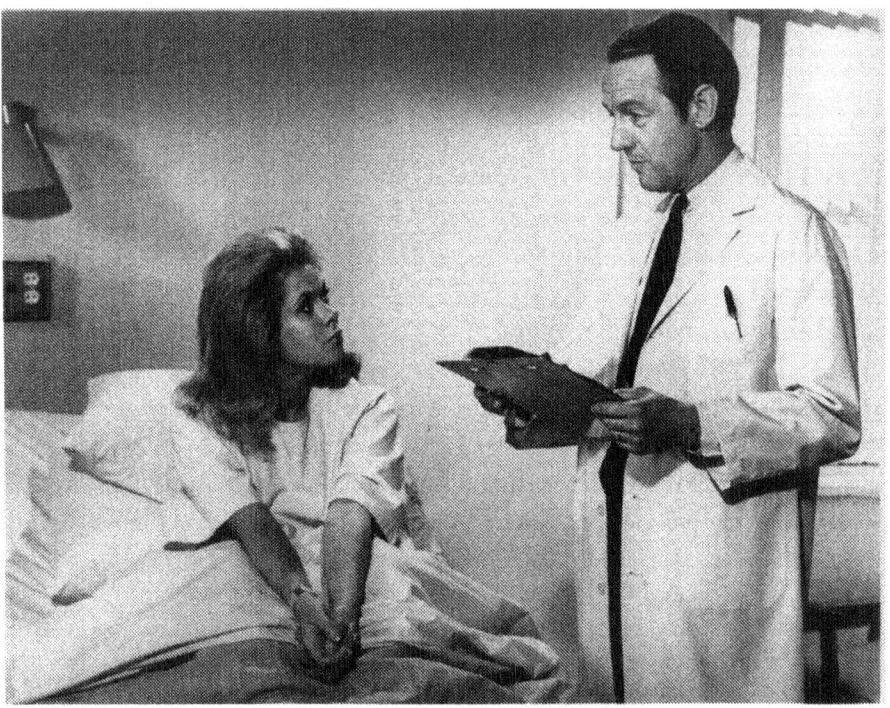

It is revealed in Episode #174, "Samantha's Curious Cravings", that Louise Tate had cravings for pizza when she was pregnant.

Also revealed in this episode is the fact that Endora had cravings for hummingbird wings when she was pregnant.

"The average American eats Italian food at least once a week."—Larry Tate, speaking to an Italian client. Episode #110, "Business, Italian Style."

Louise Tate Pizza
1 cup Marinara Sauce
1 cup shredded mozzarella cheese
1/4 teaspoon dried oregano
2 Tablespoons grated Parmesan cheese

Directions: preheat oven to 450 degrees. Prepare pizza dough. Spread marinara sauce over the dough, then sprinkle with mozzarella cheese, oregano, and Parmesan cheese. Bake pizza for 30 minutes or until crust is well browned.

Dough
1 envelope of dry yeast
2 cups lukewarm water
4 cups flour
1/2 Tablespoon of sugar
1/2 Tablespoon of salt
1/8 teaspoon pepper
1/8 cup of olive oil

Directions: in a small bowl empty contents of yeast package and add 1/4 cup of lukewarm water and stir. Next, in a larger bowl, add yeast and lukewarm water with the dry ingredients and as much as the remaining warm water that is needed. Make sure the

"I'm sick of simmering like a watched pot. I want to get out and boil."—Serena

90   The Magic of Bewitched Cookbook

Samantha has a witch disease and Samantha finds herself speaking in rhyme one morning. Endora calls upon Dr. Bombay who is busy climbing Mount Everest. He uses his Amber Corpuscular Evaluator and diagnoses her as having Secondary Vocabularyitis. His cure doesn't last, though he thinks he has cured her with a sound wave injection. Some of Samantha's food related rhymes include: "I'll be back in a jiffy, dinner was spiffy." "Eat your eggs, they're good for your legs." "You bet I am, would you like some jam?"

BREAKFAST

"Boil and bubble, toil and trouble, Mother, get here on the double."—Samantha

"Don't bust your broom."—Serena to Samantha
"That good, good morning flavor that makes getting out of bed worthwhile." (Angel Coffee)

Bewitching Fact:
Eggs benedict is one of Darrin's favorite breakfast dishes, he also likes waffles.

Endora always has fried raven's eggs over easy for breakfast. (Revealed in Episode #118, "Allergic to Macedonian Dodo Birds".)

In Episode #201, "To Go or Not To Go", Darrin looks for Endora under his breakfast plate.

Waffles
It is revealed in Episodes #138 and #148 that Darrin likes waffles for breakfast.

While serving waffles to Uncle Arthur, Samantha asks Arthur if he would like syrup. Arthur: "Yes, gobs of it!"

In the beginning of the Bewitched series, Samantha was an inexperienced cook. Samantha accidentally burnt pieces of toast, overcook eggs, turn coffee into molasses. Trying to be encouraging, Darrin has said to Samantha, "Doesn't that look good?"

"Cooking for Darrin is a pleasure."—Samantha as said to Endora in Episode #2, "Be It Ever So Mortgaged."

"Want me to fix breakfast?"—Naomi

Adam's Apple Crisp
5 medium apples, sliced thin, Pippin or Granny Smith variety
½ cup yellow cake mix
¼ cup sugar and cinnamon combination
¼ cup melted butter

Directions: place sliced apples in a glass cooking dish, sprinkle in cake mix, as well as cinnamon sugar mixture. Pour melted margarine over the mixture. Bake for 25 minutes at 400 degrees. "Here mother, have an apple, it'll keep the witch doctor away."—Samantha

Eggs Benedict
3 English muffins
6 slices broiled ham
6 poached eggs
Hollandaise Sauce

Directions: split and toast English muffins. Cut ham and place on the English muffin, slip egg on top of ham and smother with hollandaise sauce. Serve hot. Makes 6.

Eggs Benedict

In #167, "Daddy Does His Thing", Maurice turns Darrin into a donkey because Maurice feels that Darrin is acting stubborn for refusing to accept a magical lighter as a gift. Samantha eventually finds her father in Paris, and when she returns, she learns Darrin the donkey has been taken to an animal shelter. Eventually, Darrin is released and Maurice turns Darrin back into a human.

Early on in the episode, Gladys Kravitz witnesses Samantha feeding eggs benedict to a mule, and she goes straight home to tell Abner about the incident.

Gladys to Abner: "I tell you it is a jackass and she is feeding it Eggs Benedict for breakfast."

Abner: "Lucky jackass—all I ever get is lumpy oatmeal."

In "Daddy Does His Thing", it is mentioned that Eggs Benedict is one of Darrin's favorite breakfasts.

Also in Episode #167, "Daddy Does His Thing", Samantha is seen talking to baby Adam while making French toast. "We're gonna make French toast. Well, it isn't French and it isn't toast. So, that gives you an idea of what your gonna be up against in this world." Maurice materializes and has his taste buds set for something more exotic such as eggs Florentine.

Eggs Florentine
1 package, 10 ounces of chopped frozen spinach
¼ cup of butter or margarine
2 Tablespoons of flour
2 cups of half and half
8 eggs poached
Shredded Cheddar cheese and grated Parmesan cheese
Salt and pepper to taste

Directions: poach eggs and cook frozen spinach according to the package instructions. To prepare the white sauce, melt the butter or margarine in a saucepan, add flour, stir in the half and half. Stir the mixture often, making sure it becomes bubbly. Next, place the spinach in a lightly buttered shallow baking dish. Arrange eggs over the top of the spinach, then pour white sauce over eggs. Sprinkle cheese over the mixture, and, if desired, salt and pepper. Bake in a 400 degree oven for 3 minutes, until cheese is melted.

"I don't have time to eat breakfast honey."—Darrin

"Millions of women cope with pancakes in the everyday normal way, why can't you!"—Darrin

Pancakes

In #98, "Art for Sam's Sake", Samantha is in a hurry to catch the morning light to work on her painting, so she flips the pancakes via witchcraft (as in #131) and also pours the coffee the same way (#98).

Orvis, one of the dog men from the Planet Parenthia in Episode #137, "Samantha's Secret Saucer", believes that pancakes without syrup are ridiculous.

Samantha's Secret Saucer Pancakes
1 egg
1 cup buttermilk
2 Tablespoons shortening, melted
1 cup flour
1 Tablespoon sugar
1 teaspoon baking powder
1/2 teaspoon soda
1/2 teaspoon salt

Directions: place all ingredients in order listed in a bowl and beat until smooth. Pour batter (double the size of a silver dollar) onto hot griddle or skillet. Turn pancakes (or flip them via witchcraft as seen in #98, #131) as soon as they are puffed and full of bubbles. Bake on other side until golden brown.*don't forget to spray the skillet or pan with cooking spray.

Blueberry Pancakes

In #97, "I Remember You Sometimes", Samantha is seen fixing hot cakes with blueberries for Darrin's breakfast.

Darrin: "You fixed these once before."
Samantha: "No, I don't think so."
Darrin: "It was September the 14th, raining, Saturday, you were wearing the yellow dress with the white polka dots … You gave it away to Mrs. Dumont, for the rummage sale … and remember that enormous chocolate cake you whipped up by witchcraft."
Darrin is heard saying in Episode #30, that blueberry pancakes is his favorite breakfast.

Blueberry Pancakes
1 cup fresh, frozen, or canned blueberries
1 well beaten egg
1 cup milk
1/4 cup butter or margarine, melted
1 cup sifted flour
2 1/2 teaspoons baking powder
2 tablespoons sugar
3/4 teaspoon salt

Directions: drain frozen or canned blueberries thoroughly. Combine egg, milk, and butter. Sift together dry ingredients; slowly add to egg mixture, beat with an electric mixer. Brown and serve. Makes 8.

Tales of Toadstools and Barstools Madison Avenue Mocktails-Non-Alcoholic Beverages

"I guess the last item of business is the appointment of the chair of the refreshments committee."—Dave, Darrin's friend from Episode #23, "Red Light, Green Light."

In Episode #253, "Samantha's Witchcraft Blows a Fuse", Samantha and Darrin are dining at a Chinese Restaurant when Samantha sips Fong's Heavenly Himalayan concoction. Samantha tells

Mr. Fong, the restaurant owner, "You certainly came up with a bewitching drink." Immediately after drinking the exotic elixir, bright red stripes appear on Samantha's face.

Esmeralda beckons Dr. Bombay to create an antidote. Dr. Bombay's antidote consists of: Eye of condor, powdered snakeskin, fig newts (Dr. Bombay jokes, "That's the way the cookie crumbles"), one pint of nonfat unicorn milk, a toasted cheese sandwich on rye (Dr. Bombay mentions, "That's for me, I'm starved."), the tail feather from a dodo bird, and a Himalayan cinnamon stick.

Unfortunately, Dr. Bombay forgot to mention the tail feather of a dodo bird. Near the end of the episode, when Bombay finally retrieves the final ingredient, Samantha is cured.

***Bewitched* Berry Banana OJ Fizzle**
Orange Juice
1 Banana
7-up or Sprite
Strawberry soda
Optional: ice

Directions: Combine orange juice, sliced banana, 7-Up and strawberry soda in a punch bowl. You may also do a variation of this Bewitching concoction by placing all ingredients in a blender and adding some ice.

Pineapple Dream
Orange juice
Pineapple juice
7-UP or Sprite soda
Lime to garnish
Optional: ice

Directions: Mix all ingredients in a punch bowl, serve.

Fuzz Doll
Orange juice
7-UP or Sprite
Optional: ice

Directions: Mix all ingredients in a punch bowl, serve. To make this drink for one, use a can of Sprite or 7-Up, and ½ cup of Orange Juice.

Strawberry Mango Pucker
Strawberry Mango juice
Lemonade
Lime to garnish

Directions: Mix all ingredients in a punch bowl, serve.

Razzdango
Red raspberry
Mango juice
7-Up or Sprite

Directions: Mix all ingredients in a punch bowl, serve.

Witches Brew
3 cups apricot nectar
3 cups pineapple or orange juice
4 cups ginger ale or 7-up
2 cups orange or lemon sherbet

Directions: In a large bowl, combine the apricot and pineapple juices. Just before serving, add the chilled ginger ale. Pour into glasses and top with tiny scoops of sherbet.

Darrin caters to Samantha with hot tea or iced tea in "Samantha's Better Halves".
Tea Recipe
¾ cup of instant tea
2/3 cup lemonade mix with sugar

½ cup instant orange drink such as Tang
1 teaspoon ground allspice
½ teaspoon cloves

Directions: Combine ingredients and mix thoroughly. Stir in one Tablespoon of mix per cup of water. Makes 1 ¾ cups of mix.

Cherry Punch
1 can (6 ounces) frozen lemonade concentrate, thawed
1 can (6 ounces) frozen limeade concentrate, thawed
1 can (20 ounces) pineapple chunks, undrained
2 cups of water
2 liters of cherry soda, chilled
2 liters of ginger ale, chilled
Sliced lemon and lime slices

Directions: in a blender, mix concentrates as well as pineapple, until smooth. Next, stir in water. In a punch bowl, add sodas and frozen pineapple mixture. Garnish with lemon and lime slices.

Raspberry Pineapple Punch
One 10 ounce package of frozen raspberries in syrup, thawed
4 cups of pineapple juice
One six ounce can of frozen lemonade concentrate, thawed
One bottle of 7-Up
Ice cubes
Lemon or lime slices for garnish

Directions: In a punch bowl add thawed raspberries, lemonade concentrate and the other remaining ingrients. Garnish with lemon or lime slices, or both.

Dick Albain, props man on Bewitched, with Agnes Moorehead and Elizabeth Montgomery. Mark Simpson Collection.

Witch's Brew Too!
1 14oz. can of sweetened condensed milk
1 46oz. can pineapple juice, chilled
1 2-liter bottle of orange soda, chilled
Orange sherbet ice cream.

Directions: in a punch bowl, or a clean jack o'lantern container, stir together sweetened condensed milk, pineapple juice, and orange soda. Top with sherbet and serve over ice.

*One of Dr. Bombay's potions contains, marrow from a saber-tooth tiger, eye of newt, toe of frog, wool of bat, and dietetic cola.

Fingerful Punch
2 cans of red concentrated red punch
1 liter of 7-up or Lemon Lime Soda
2 latex gloves

Directions: fill two latex gloves with water and tie off the ends with a rubber band and place into the freezer. In a punch bowl, mix 7-up with 2 cans of red punch, add water according to the punch directions. When the latex gloves are frozen, take the "hand" out of the glove and add to the punch bowl. You will have floating hands, and it will also serve to keep the punch cold.

Rollos Love Potion
1 Quart of Lemonade
Pop rocks, the popping candy
Honey for sticking

Directions: Put about 1 Tablespoon of honey into a shallow teacup saucer or a paper plate. Next, dip the rims of a tall glasse into the honey. On a separate plate, sprinkle pop rocks. When the tall glass is ready with the honey mixture, take the pop rocks off the plate and sprinkle on the sides making sure it sticks to the honey. Last, carefully take the lemonade in a separate pitcher and pour into the glass.

Darrin's cousin Helen is smitten with Prince Charming, thinking he is Samantha's cousin Charlie, she pursues Charlie and one morning when Endora answers the door, Helen says, "Do you mind if I have a cup of Charlie. Oh, I mean coffee." From Episode #129, "A Prince of a Guy".

Cup of Charlie
Coffee Maker
Paper filter for coffee maker (make sure it is the correct size for the specific coffee maker)
French Roast gourmet Coffee
Coffee grinder

Directions: In a coffee grinder place the desired amount of beans for brewing and grind. Next, place freshly ground coffee in paper filter in the coffee maker. Next, add water to coffee maker, the more water the weaker the coffee will be. The less water, the stronger the coffee will be. Turn on coffee maker and wala, in a few minutes a cup of Charlie. May add sugar or creamer or store bought vanilla creamer to coffee.

"If I'm not telling the truth, may I never enjoy another wolf bane on the the rocks."—Endora

Wolf bane On the rocks Orange Julius
1/2 cup of orange juice, without pulp
1/2 cup of sunny delight
1 Tablespoon of Vanilla Extract
¾ cup of ice
1 Tablespoon of Granulated Sugar

Directions: In a blender place all of the ingredients. Blend on medium speed until ice has been crushed and Julius is frothy. May add more ice and or orange juice as needed.

Cocktails

"I only had tee martoonies."–Darrin from *No Zip in my Zap* Episode.

In Episode #1, "I Darrin, Take This Witch Samantha", this scene happens on their honeymoon.

"I wish I had a drink."—Darrin
A glass magically appears in his hand.
"An Old Fashioned?"—Darrin
"What about a straw?"—Darrin
Straw pops in the drink.

"You're a witch!"—Darrin to Samantha
"That's what I've been trying to tell you!"—Samantha

Darrin: "My wife's a witch. What'll I do?"
Bartender:" You ought to see my wife."

Here are a few drinks that Darrin might have consumed at Joe's Bar and Grill

In Episode #105, "*Bewitched*, Bothered, and infuriated", Mr. Murray, the hotel manager says this as a reaction to seeing a manifestation of witchcraft.

Mr. Murray: "I've got to stop hitting that brandy after dinner." "No more Bloody Mary's at breakfast either." I've got to get a complete checkup, and the sooner the better!"

"Just make yourself comfortable."—Samantha "I will, just as soon as you show me where the bar is."–Mr. Saunders, Client

Cocktails at 5:00

One of Darrin's coping mechanisms to deal with the mayhem would be to retreat to Joe's Bar and Grill. He often would tell his woes to a lonely drunkard.

Darrin: "My wife's a witch, my mother-in-law is a witch, I'm Surrounded by them."
Drunk: "You ought to see my mother-in-law, she has fangs."
(Samantha pops into the bar)
Samantha: "Darrin, are you coming home?"
Darrin: "No."
Drunk: "Well, she doesn't look like a witch to me!"
Darrin: "Well, she is!!!"

Eventually, in his inebriated state, he would find his way home.

Darrin: Good evening, Samantha. Good evening, madam.
Sam: Darrin?
Darrin: Don't you recognize me either?
Sam: What's wrong?
Endora: He's sauced to the gill.
Sam: Mother, please!
Darrin: Nonsense, madam, I'm quite sober. I only had tee martinis.
Sam: Well, you better take the olives out of your mouth because you're talking funny.

Endora:	Funny is better than dreary.
Darrin:	Would you kindly tell little Miss Muffet to get her tuffet out of here!
Endora:	All right, but if you need me, just light a match near his breath. I'll see the flames.
Darrin:	Good old Smokey the Bore.

Clients

It should be noted that Darrin was not the only character on *Bewitched* who drank excessively—clients, as well as Larry Tate, were known to booze it up. Larry often invited guests/clients over to the Stephens' house not only to drink, but to partake in dinner as well as dessert, often at the last minute! Viewers didn't see too many clients over at the Tate's residence with Louise slaving in the kitchen to make everything just perfect for the clients. "In Episode #53, "Maid to Order", bumbling maid Naomi is looking for work so she can give her son money to make it through medical school. She is hired temporarily by Samantha and Darrin until Tabitha is born. Larry and Louise come to dinner one night, and Samantha helps Naomi magically with her cooking duties. Louise and Larry later hire Naomi for a dinner party and there is worry on the part of Louise that the food isn't turning out right. Alls well that ends well, and Samantha realizes cooking and cleaning are not Naomi's' forte, rather accounting.

In Episode #238, "Hansel and Gretel in Samantha land", there is more mayhem as there is a witch running around the Stephens' home who wants to eat little children. (From the classic fairy tale of Hansel and Gretel)

Louise:	"I think there's something radically wrong here."
Larry:	"Only if they run out of Scotch."
Witch:	"Poor dear was wandering around in the woods lost and grandma put her in the guest room."
Samantha:	"Why don't you two have a little drink before din?" (Larry suddenly is asleep on the couch)
Louise:	"I don't think Larry needs another drink."
Later, Larry says:	"This is the first time in my life I've had a hangover before dinner."

"I thought it would be nice to make a toast to the new company."—Samantha

It would be difficult to watch Bewitched and not to notice the amount of alcohol consumed. Perhaps one of my favorite alcohol related incidents is with Mary The Good Fairy played by actress Imogene Coca. She is tired and cold, and wants to rest awhile, she locates a witch's home, and decides that she'll hang up her fairy wings for a time and relax. Mary complains of being chilly and Samantha offers tea or coffee, the only thing that seems to interest Mary is the mention of Brandy by Darrin. Mary drinks the unfamiliar concoction quickly and requests another, when Samantha goes to the kitchen to make Mary a sandwich, Mary convinces Darrin to give her more brandy and in no time, the beloved tooth fairy is crocked. Mary is unable to perform her tooth fairy duties and Samantha takes over temporarily.

"How about a nice cup of tea"—Samantha

"I certainly could use something to warm me up, but I don't know about tea though."—Mary, the Good Fairy

"Coffee?"—Samantha

"No, coffee doesn't agree with me."—Mary, the Good Fairy

"How about a drop of brandy?"—Darrin

"What's brandy?"—Mary, the Good Fairy

"It's a very good warmer upper."—Samantha

"Oh, then that certainly should agree with me."—Mary, the Good Fairy

Trivia Tidbit:

Barstools and Toadstools, Listed below are some of the names of the bars that Darrin retreated to.

Elbow Room Cocktail Lounge
Golden Spoon
Hearthstone Bar
Happy Times Bar
Joe's Bar and Grill
Purple Popsicle Night Club
Dundee's Bar
Diamond Slipper

Increments

In Episode #161, a huge wine glass is used as a prop. In "Marriage, Witches Style," Serena thinks she is meeting a nice, simple mortal guy and later realizes that she has attracted a snobby warlock by the name of Franklyn Blodgett. Franklyn untactful likens Serena's witchcraft move to resembling a demented windmill." While Franklyn is giving Serena advice on how to use witchcraft with finesse, Serena zaps up a jumbo wine glass, floats it above his head and pours the drink all over him.

Increments
1 cup
8 ounces
1 split
6.3 ounces
1 wineglass
4 ounces
1 pony
1 ounce
1 dash 1/32 ounce
1 jigger
1 ½ ounces

Types of Glasses
Collins
Champagne
Cocktail
Double Rocks
Hurricane
Goblet
Highball
Martini
Double Rocks

Sour
Old Fashioned

"If you're going to fly, don't drink."—Darrin as said to Mary the Good Fairy

White Witch
1/2 lime
1/2 ounce white crème de cacao
1/2 ounce cointreau
1 ounce white Jamaica rum
Club Soda

Directions: Squeeze lime juice into a glass filled with ice cubes; save Lime shell. Add to glass crème de cacao, cointreau, and rum. Add Club soda to fill glass. Stir. Decorate with lime shell and fresh Mint dusted with bar sugar.

In Episode #130, "McTavish", Darrin has been drinking and he says to Samantha,
"If I had any vision, I would realize that you can't take a proud bird born to ride the wings of the wind to live in the sparkle of a star, and pen it up in a domestic coop and expect it to walk around with a smile on its beak!"
Samantha: "Darrin, have you been drinking?"
Darrin then says, "Everything is very clear." Your mother has been right all along." Samantha, "Darrin, you have been drinking!"

Zombie
Juice of 1/2 lime
1 1/2 ounces orange juice
1 ounce lemon juice
1/4 ounce grenadine

Scotch & Water
Pour 1 to 1 1/2 ounces scotch over ice cubes in a 14-ounce
Highball glass. Serve a small pitcher of water alongside. Great drink for entertaining with clients.

In Episode #167, "Daddy Does His Thing", Samantha expresses concern because Darrin is thirsty and wants his water in a bucket. Maurice earlier in the episode turned Darrin into a donkey.

"After midnight everybody, time for bloody Mary's."—Samantha

Bloody Mary
One 46 ounce bottle of chilled tomato juice
3 tablespoons horseradish
3 tablespoons of freshly squeezed lemon juice
1 teaspoon of Tabasco sauce
¾ of a teaspoon of Worcestershire sauce
1 ½ cups of vodka
Ice cubes

Directions: In a large pitcher, combine tomato juice, lemon juice, Tabasco, horseradish, Worcestershire, and vodka. Stir until well blended. Next, fill 8–10 glasses with mixture, adding ice, a lemon wedge or celery stalk. May sprinkle with pepper.

Endora throws a Halloween bash at the Stephens' home. Ecto, the invisible butler tells her that they have run out of champagne. Endora informs Ecto that there are two more cases on the service porch.

Time for a Party Punch
(A favorite recipe of the late Mildred Ferrari)
6 ounces concentrated orange juice, thawed
2 cans pineapple juice
1 cup lemon juice
1 cup sugar
Champagne
Chablis wine

Directions: Mix and keep cold. Just before serving, add 2 bottles of champagne and 1 bottle of chilled Chablis.

In Episode #21, "Ling Ling", Samantha changes a cat into an Asian woman named Ling Ling to help Darrin for an advertising campaign. Darrin's friend Wally is the photographer for the shoot and falls for Ling Ling. Wally learns that Ling Ling is truly catty when she chooses cat nip over him.

Nine Lives
½ ounce of rum
½ ounce of dry vermouth
½ ounce of gin
½ ounce of sloe gin
½ ounce of triple sec
½ ounce of vodka
½ ounce of whiskey
6 ounces of coke a cola or Hawaiian Punch

Directions: In shaker with ice, add the ingredients, strain. Add a cherry with a pineapple or Orange slice as garnish.

Gin and Tonic
Tonic Water
A shot of Gin
A twist of lemon or lime

*My husband David's favorite drink. He says it has to be good, it is only one letter off from my name. Gin (Gina)

Wicked Gin and Tonic
That's what they call them on the East Coast. It's Darrin Stephens and Larry Tate's favorite libation.
Fill glass with ice
1 shot Gin or Vodka
Directions: Remainder of glass, fill with Tonic water
Enjoy!

*Darrin believes that Endora brings a "black cloud" whenever she pops in at the Stephens residence.

Black Cloud
1 part vodka
1 part Tia Maria

Directions: Stir with ice cubes. Strain into chilled cocktail glass.

Dr. Bombay's two favorite sure to cure home remedy drinks

In Episode #42, "Take Two Aspirin and Half a Pint of Porpoise Milk", Samantha becomes ill after having contact with a black Peruvian rose. A mortal doctor decides her health is fine, but Dr. Bombay must find a cure. This is the first witch-illness show shown on *Bewitched*.

Bombay Cocktail
1/2 ounce French vermouth
1/2 ounce Italian vermouth
1 ounce brandy
1/4 ounce Per nod
1/2 teaspoon Curacao

Directions: Stir well with ice cubes. Strain into 3-ounce cocktail glass.

Bombay Punch
1 quart brandy
1 quart sweet sherry
4 ounces maraschino liqueur
1/2 pint Curacao
4 quarts champagne
2 quarts club soda
Sliced fresh fruits
Halved seeded grapes

Directions: Pre chill all liquid ingredients. Pour into punch bowl embedded In cracked ice. Add fruits. Serve in champagne glasses. Serves 35 to 40 people.

*In Episode #244, "Samantha Is Earthbound", Dr Bombay pulls martini mix, lime juice, and instant Manhattan mix out of his doctor's bag. While he is doing this, the tune of "I'll Take Manhattan" plays in the background.

"One drink and look out."—Endora getting Serena drunk, Corsican Cousins

Manhattan
1 ½ ounces of blended whiskey
½ ounce of sweet vermouth

Directions: Place whiskey and sweet vermouth in a shaker with ice and strain. For a dry Manhattan, use dry vermouth and garnish with an olive.

118　The Magic of Bewitched Cookbook

In Episode #233, *"Bewitched*, Bothered, & Baldoni", Endora makes the statue of Venus come to life to test Darrin's love for Samantha. To counteract Venus's (named Vanessa in the episode) affect over men, Samantha brings to life Adonis, the God of love.

Adonis Cocktail
1 ounce sweet sherry
1/2 ounce Italian vermouth
1 dash orange bitters

Directions: Shake with ice cubes. Strain into chilled cocktail glass.
*While in Rome, Endora brings to life the statue of Venus, The Goddess Of love, to test Darrin's affection for Samantha. To counteract Endora's spell, Samantha brings to life the statue of Adonis, the God of Love.

In "Paris, Witches' Style", Maurice discovers that Samantha has been traveling in Europe sans (without) her daddy. Maurice is angered at his daughters' travels without him and seeks to punish Darrin, whom he believes is to blame. Endora creates an alternative Darrin who is pleasant to Maurice. However, Maurice discovers the fraudulent Darrin and zooms the real Darrin directly to the top of the Eiffel Tower. Darrin's client, Mr. Sagan, believes it is a publicity campaign.

120   The Magic of Bewitched Cookbook

French Cocktail
2 ounces Per nod
1/2 lump sugar

Directions: Half fill cocktail glass with shaved ice. Place sugar on top. Drip Per nod on sugar. Add a twist of lemon peel, and serve with Cut straws.

Cafe de Paris Cocktail For Episode #234, "Paris, Witches Style"
1 1/2 ounces gin
1 egg white
1 teaspoon Per nod or Herb saint
1 teaspoon fresh cream

Directions: Shake well with ice cubes. Strain into chilled 4-ounces cocktail Glass.
*Maurice is angered to find out that Samantha and Darrin are in Europe without his knowledge or consent. He takes his wrath out on Darrin, and eventually zaps Darrin to the top of the Eiffel Tower. Darrin's client, Mr. Sagan, thinks the Eiffel Tower event is a stunt for his campaign. All is well that ends well and Darrin gets the account.

Champs Elysees Cocktail
1 ounce cognac
1/4 ounce green Chartreuse
1 teaspoon lemon juice
2 drops Angostura bitters

Directions: Shake with ice cubes. Strain into chilled cocktail glass

Cuba Libre
1 ounce of Rum
Coke or Pepsi
Lime as garnish

Directions: Fill a glass with ice cubes and coke or Pepsi soda. Squeeze lime into the glass, Add the rum, and stir.

Rum and Coke
1 ounce of Rum
Coke or Pepsi

Directions: Add ice cubes to a glass. Next, add coke or Pepsi and rum. Stir. If sugar Content is of concern, you may use diet Coke or diet Pepsi. For an added zing, Use flavored colas such as Vanilla or Cherry Coke.

Queen Victoria Crown and Coke
1 ounce of Crown Rum
Coca Cola

Directions: Add ice cubes to a glass. Next, add the coke and Crown Rum. Stir.

Country Club Collins
Tall glass, filled with ice
2 ounces of Sweet and Sour
1 ounce of Chambord.

Directions: Fill the glass with club soda Add Chambord and Sweet and Sour. May add cherries as a garnish.

Absinthe Italiano Cocktail for Episode #110, "Business, Italian Style"
1 ounce absinthe
1/2 ounce anisette
3 dashed maraschino liqueur
1/4 ounce water

Directions: Shake with ice cubes. Strain into chilled cocktail glass. Serve with Ice-water chaser.
*Darrin is eager to learn Italian to impress a client. Endora casts a spell that makes Darrin only speak Italian. This causes quite a mess as Darrin is stripped of the English language, and the client, Mr. Romani, thinks Darrin is mocking the Italian language.

"I want you to know, I've had a perfectly bourbon time."—Mr. Saunders (from Episode #106, "Nobody but a Frog Knows How to Live."

Bourbon
2 ounces of Bourbon Whiskey
4 ounces of lemon-lime soda
1 lemon wedge, sliced

Directions: Pour the bourbon and soda into a highball glass almost filled to the top with ice cubes. Stir and add the lemon wedge.

Trivia Tidbit:

In Episode #168, "Samantha's Good News", we find out that Samantha is pregnant with Adam. In real life, Elizabeth Montgomery gave birth to a daughter whom they named Rebecca Elizabeth Montgomery. Coincidentally enough, Rebecca was born on Erin Murphy's (Tabitha) fifth birthday, June 17, 1969. Maurice hears of the impending birth via Sam's aura being zonked across the Atmospheric Continuum. In this episode, he says he hasn't seen his wife Endora for two or three months, well, maybe it has been eighteen or so months.

Tickled Pink

(Samantha and Darrin have just had little Tabitha. Let's celebrate By making this yummy tickled pink punch)

½ gallon of raspberry sherbet
2 bottles of pink champagne
2 cans of 7-Up
¼ cup of vodka

In #188, "Samantha's Secret Is Discovered", Samantha transports herself and says, "Elixir of herbs and slow gin fizz, whisk me to where Mrs. Stephens is. Oh, that's terrible!"

Pink Cloud

3/4 ounce evaporated milk
3/4 ounce white crème de cacao
3/4 ounce Crème de Noyaux

Directions: Shake with ice cubes.

*Tabitha was born in Episode #54, "And Then There Were Three", on January 13, 1966. Darrin believes that Endora has turned his new born daughter into an adult woman. It turns out to be Samantha's look-a-like cousin Serena.

Trivia Tidbit:

At the time *Bewitched* aired, California law mandated that children could only work for a few hours per day. Shooting often ran between 12 and 14 hours per day. That is the reasoning why Tabitha and Adam were played by twins.

Platinum Blonde

1 ounce Barbados rum
1 ounce Grand Marnier
1/2 ounce fresh cream

Directions: Shake with ice cubes. Strain into chilled cocktail glass.

White Cloud
3/4 ounce vodka
1/2 ounce white crème de cacao
1 dash evaporated milk
1 dash Lopez coconut cream

Directions: Shake with ice cubes. Strain into chilled lady cocktail glass.
*Samantha and Endora often retreat to Cloud #8 or Cloud #9.

Maurice was on the planet Venus while Endora gave birth Samantha on the eve of the Galactic Rejuvenation and Dinner Dance. Episode #175, "And Something Makes Four."

Around the World
3 ounces orange juice
3 ounces lemon juice
3 ounces light Puerto Rican rum
1/2 ounce brandy
Juice of 1/2 fresh lime

Directions: Blend with 2 scoops of shaved ice for 12 to 15 seconds in electric Mixer. Pour into 2 grapefruit supreme glasses. Fill glasses With cracked ice. Serve with straws. Makes 2 drinks.

*Endora, Maurice, Serena, and Dr. Bombay are free-spirits who often travel around the world. However, they usually vacation separately.

Aunt Agatha
1 1/2 ounces light Puerto Rican rum
2 ounces orange juice
Angostura bitters

Directions: Pour rum and orange juice over ice cubes in old fashioned glass. Stir. Float a few drops of bitters on top.

Mary the Good Fairy Brandy
1 ounce of Brandy
1 ounce of Crème de Cacao
1 ounce of heavy cream
½ cup of ice

Directions: Combine all ingredients in a blender. Blend for about a minute. Top with cocoa powder, cinnamon, or nutmeg, or a combination of the three.

Imogene Coca as Mary the Good Fairy. Mark Simpson Collection.

Boston Cooler The Stephens visited Massachusetts in Episode #202, 203, 204, 205, 206, 207, & 208.
Juice of 1/2 lemon
1/4 teaspoon sugar
2 ounces of New England rum
Club soda

Directions: Shake lemon juice, sugar, and rum with ice cubes. Strain into a Goblet. Add ice cubes. Fill with soda. Add a dash of rum on top.

* In Episode # 201, "To Go or Not to Go, That is the Question", Endora wants Samantha to attend a witches' convention in Salem, Massachusetts, but Sam won't go unless Darrin is invited. In Episode #206, "Paul Revere Rides Again", Esmeralda accidentally zaps up Paul Revere, the famous Bostonian who warned the Patriots that the British soldiers were coming to attack. In this episode, Paul and his horse appear in the Stephens' hotel room. Darrin convinces a client that Paul is part of an advertising campaign.

Trivia Tidbit:
Cable network TV Land erected a 9 foot bronze statue of Samantha Stephens that is in Lappin Park which is located in Salem, Massachusetts.

Bourbon Highball
2 ounces Bourbon
Ginger ale

Directions: Pour Bourbon over ice cubes in a highball glass. Fill with ginger ale. Add a twist of lemon peel. Stir.

Highball
2 ounces brandy
Ginger ale or club soda

Directions: Pour brandy over 1 ice cube in an 8-ounce highball glass. Fill with ginger ale or club soda. Add a twist of lemon peel. Stir gently.

Horse's Highball
4 ounces brandy
2 dashes Per nod
3 dashes Angostura bitters
1 teaspoon lemon juice
1 teaspoon sugar syrup
1 egg
Club soda

Directions: Shake all ingredients except soda with ice cubes. strain into tall highball glasses. Add ice cubes. Fill glass with soda. Dust with grated nutmeg.

*In Episodes #61, "The Horse's Mouth" and #241, "Three Men and a Witch on a Horse", Samantha changes a horse into a human.

Can you name the racehorse turned human in Episode #61?
A. Dolly
B. Molly
C. Golly

In "Three Men and a Witch on a Horse", Endora casts a spell on Darrin, what does the spell do?

Answers: A. Dolly, turns Darrin into a gambler

Trivia Tidbit:

Elizabeth Montgomery adored going to the horse races with her grandmother Rebecca. Elizabeth and Bill Asher named their only daughter, Rebecca, after Liz's grandmother.

Erin Murphy, in April of 2005, went on Entertainment Tonight and stated that Elizabeth Montgomery enjoyed gambling and had a penchant for making horse bets.

Morning Glory Margaritas
(Makes 8–10 margaritas)
1 lime, cut into 8–10 wedges
8–10 toothpicks
8–10 maraschino cherries
1 pint of Tequila
1 cup of orange liqueur, such as Triple Sec
1 cup freshly squeezed lime juice
Ice cubes
Rock (coarse salt), to rim the margarita glasses

Directions: In a pie tin, place salt. Rub the rims of the margarita glasses with lime juice (may use lemon juice). Dip the rims of each glass into the salt. Next, combine the tequila, orange liqueur, lime juice and ice into a blender. Blend the mixture. On a toothpick, place cherry and small lime wedge. Pour into the margarita glasses and garnish with lime and a cherry.

For a sweeter margarita, add flavoring, such as strawberry and rim the glass with sugar.

Trivia Tidbit:
Episode #170, "Samantha and Darrin in Mexico City", was Dick York's last appearance on *Bewitched*.

Clover Leaf Cocktail

*Darrin's parents are Irish and this is their favorite drink.

1 1/2 ounces gin
4 dashes grenadine
Juice of 1/2 lime or lemon
1 egg white

Directions: Shake with ice cubes. Strain into a chilled double cocktail glass. Decorate with a mint leaf.

Irish coffee
4 ounces hot coffee
3 cocktail sugar cubes
1 ounce Irish whisky
2 ounces heavy cream, slightly whipped

Directions: Stir coffee, sugar, and whiskey in a preheated fizz or Tahitian Coffee glass. Float cream on top.

There are a few episodes about Leprechauns. In Episode #63, "The Leprechaun", Samantha tries to help a leprechaun recover his lost pot of gold. In Episode #197, "If The Shoe Pinches," Endora interferes in her daughter's life by sending a leprechaun to her house. The leprechaun gives Darrin a pair of custom made shoes. According to legend, it is bad luck not to accept a gift from a Leprechaun. The shoes make Darrin lazy and disinterested in working. In one scene, Larry says to Samantha, "Is he drunk?" "No, Larry, he isn't."—Samantha. "Work is a sickness with you."—Darrin "Yes, but it obviously isn't contagious."—Larry

Moonlight For Episode #91, "Sam in the Moon." Darrin cannot understand why Samantha does not want to watch news telecast of the moon. As it turns out, she has been there before.

Juice of 1 lemon
1/2 tablespoon bar sugar
2 ounces calvados or applejack
Club soda

Directions: Shake lemon juice, sugar, and calvados with ice cubes. Strain into a Highball glass. Add 1 ice cube. Fill glass with soda. Decorate with Sliced fresh fruit.

Country Club Cooler for Episode #164, "The Battle of Burning Oak". Darrin is asked to become a member of a very snooty country club. Endora places a spell on Darrin that turns him into a snob. Samantha discovers that many of the members have less than perfect family backgrounds. As a result, the club relaxes its rules concerning admittance.
One of the statements that makes the Burning Oak set reconsider its stance is stated by Samantha, "The only true American is the American Indian, and you would never allow an Indian in."

1/2 teaspoon grenadine
Club soda or ginger ale
2 ounces French vermouth
Spiral-cut lemon or orange peel

Directions: Stir grenadine and 2 ounces soda or ginger ale together in a 12-ounce glass. Fill glass with ice cubes. Add vermouth. Fill with soda or ginger ale, and stir again. Insert lemon or orange spiral, and dangle end over rim of glass.

Country Club Collins
1 ounce of Chambord
2 ounces of Sweet and sour

Directions: Fill the glass with club soda and add ice. May garnish with lime and a cherry.

Morning Glory The Stephens' address is 1164 Morning Glory Circle, located in Westport, Connecticut

2 ounces of Scotch or Bourbon
2 dashes Per nod
1 egg white
1 teaspoon bar sugar
Juice of 1/2 lemon

Juice of 1/2 lime
Club soda

Directions: Shake all ingredients except soda with ice cubes. Strain into chilled large goblet. Fill glass with soda.

Holiday Eggnog
12 eggs, separated
2 cups bar sugar
1 teaspoon vanilla
1 1/2 gallons cold milk
1 pint brandy
1 cup Jamaica rum
Grated nutmeg

Directions: Beat egg yolks until thick; gradually add 1 1/2 cups of the sugar, and beat until thick and lemon colored. Beat in vanilla and milk.

Stir in brandy and rum, pouring them into milk mixture very
Slowly. With clean beaters, beat whites until soft peaks form;
Gradually add remaining sugar, and beat until whites are stiff. Spoon egg whites over the top of the milk mixture, and sprinkle with nutmeg. At serving time, ladle off a hole in the topping, ladle liquid out of This opening, and break off a spoonful of the topping with each serving of eggnog. Serves 30 to 35 people.

*Great Christmas beverage for the Stephens' guests to compliment Episodes #15, #123, #184

Trivia Tidbits:

Client Clio Vanita owns Vino Vanita Wines in Rome, Italy

Milky Way
1/2 ounce brandy
1/2 ounce Jamaica rum
1/2 ounce Bourbon
6 ounces milk
3 drops vanilla

Directions: Shake well in commercial electric drink mixer with a large scoop of ice cubes. Pour into a 10-ounce glass. Add ice cubes to almost fill glass. Dust with grated nutmeg. Serve with a straw.

Southern Comfort
Juice of 1/2 lemon
1/2 teaspoon bar sugar
2 ounces Southern Comfort
Club soda

Directions: Shake lemon juice, sugar, and Southern Comfort with ice cubes. Strain into a highball glass. Add 2 ice cubes. Fill glass with soda.

*In Episode #142, "Samantha Goes South for a Spell", Darrin must go back To Old New Orleans in the year 1868 and bring Samantha back to present day.

Golf Cocktail for Episode #114, "Birdies, Bogeys and Baxter".
1 ounce gin
1/2 ounce French vermouth
2 dashes Angostura bitters

Directions: Stir with ice cubes. Strain into chilled cocktail glass.
Add an olive.
*Endora places a spell on Darrin which makes him an excellent golfer much to the chagrin of Mr. Baxter, a client who prides himself on being a superior athlete.

Kentucky Colonel Cocktail for Episode #220, "This Little Piggie".
1/2 ounce Benedictine
1 1/2 ounce Bourbon

Directions: Stir with ice cubes. Strain into chilled cocktail glass. Add a twist of lemon peel.
*Endora turns Darrin into a pig because she thinks he is acting pigheaded. In walks Colonel Brigham (who specializes in spareribs). Endora convinces the Colonel that Darrin is modeling a way to market ribs. (See ribs recipe below)
*Note: The Colonel gets perturbed because people misinterpret what type of Colonel he is. He was a Colonel in the U.S. Army.

King George V
1/2 ounce lemon juice
1/2 ounce cointreau
1/2 ounce white crème de cacao
1/2 ounce gin
1/2 ounce scotch or Bourbon

Directions: Shake with ice cubes. Strain into chilled tiki stem champagne glass or other large saucer champagne glass.

Mai Tai
1 lime
1/2 ounce orange Curacao
1/4 ounce rock candy syrup

1 ounce dark Jamaica rum
1 ounce Martinique rum

Directions: Cut lime in half; squeeze juice over shaved ice in a mai tai glass; Save one spent shell. Add remaining ingredients and enough shaved ice to fill glass. Hand shakes. Decorate with spent lime shell, fresh mint, and a fruit stick.

"Sam, you are a witch in a million."—Darrin
Million Dollar Cocktail (For that Million Dollar Account)
2 teaspoons pineapple juice
1 teaspoon grenadine
1 egg white
3/4 ounce Italian vermouth
1 1/2 ounces gin

Directions: Shake well with ice cubes. Strain into chilled large cocktail glass.

Dry Martini
1 ounce gin
1/4 ounce French vermouth
1/2 teaspoon Per nod

Directions: Stir with ice cubes. Strain into chilled cocktail glass. decorate with a pearl cocktail onion.
*Maurice likes his martinis made with Spanish gin, Italian vermouth, and a Greek olive.

*Larry says that Louise gets mean when she drinks martinis. (Stated in "Mixed Doubles, Episode #221.

Martini Variations
Dirty Martini: Made with a few drops of olive brine.
Gin Martini: Made with a 1:1 ratio of gin and sweet vermouth.
"I'll have a martini with a twist of legs-lemon."—Larry Tate

Black and White Martini (to watch with Season 1 and Season 2 on DVD)
4 ounces of Vanilla vodka
1 ounce of Crème de cacao

Mule In Episode #167, "Daddy Does His Thing," Maurice turns Darrin into a mule.
1 1/2 ounces Vodka
Juice of 1/4 lime
7-Up

Directions: Pour vodka and lime juice over ice cubes in an old fashioned glass or glass mug. Fill glass with 7-Up.

Crazy Charlie
2 parts Vodka
1 part Gin
1 part Club Soda

Directions: Combine all ingredients in a pitcher, stir.

Irish coffee
1 ½ ounces of Irish whiskey
2 teaspoons of light brown sugar
4 ounces of hot coffee
Whipping cream

Directions: Place hot coffee in a mug. Next, add the brown sugar and Irish whiskey. With a spoon, dissolve the ingredients. Lastly, add a generous dollop of whipped cream. May add Cinnamon on top of whipping cream for an added flavor.

Lemon Drop
1 ½ ounces of plain or lemon vodka
¾ ounce of fresh lemon juice
1 teaspoon of sugar

Directions: Place lemon vodka and freshly squeezed lemon juice into a shaker with plenty of ice. Add sugar and shake. Stain into a chilled cocktail glass. Can also line the rim of the glass with lemon juice (to make it stick) and sugar.

Mother Jenny Jams Pucker Collins
½ ounce of Sour Apple Puckers
½ ounce of Peach Puckers
½ ounce of Tropical Fruit Puckers
2 ounces of sweet and sour.

Directions: Fill a glass with club soda. Next, add a cherry.
(After the accidental striptease from Aunt Clara's disappearing clothes, in Episode #44, "The Very Informal Dress", this drink will hopefully vanish.)
*not your grandmothers' jam.

"I think I'll have another drink."—Larry talking to a Toy Soldier

Toy Soldier
2 cans of fruit punch
1 pint of gin
1 pint of vodka
8 cups of ice

Directions: In a large punch bowl, combine fruit punch, gin, and vodka. Stir in the ice.

Kickapoo Joy Juice
(Made up version of the Joy Juice)
½ gallon lime sherbet
2 bottles of white champagne
2 cans of 7-Up
¼ cup of Vodka

Directions: Place 7-up, vodka and scoops of lime sherbet into a punch bowl. When ready to serve, add the white champage.

Larry Tates' Little Black Book of Hangover Remedy Cures

Larry Tate of course would never admit to having a bender every now and then. He might even request a sobriety test and admit that even when he is sober he has a hard time saying Chrysanthemum.

The best way to avoid a hangover of course is not to drink. But if you decide to partake, do so in moderation and plan to drink plenty of water the day before. Keeping your system hydrated will reduce the likelihood of getting a hangover. Also, don't skip any meals, eat a full breakfast, lunch, and dinner. A full stomach slows down the absorption of alcohol, so your body has more time to process the toxins. Having a full stomach also decreases stomach irritation, helping the drinker not to vomit. Taking multivitamins also prepares your body for the possibility of depletion of vitamins due to frequent urination while in taking alcohol.

While drinking, it is best to stick to one particular alcoholic beverage, versus mixing multiple types of drinks. Beer has the lowest concentration of alcohol (4 to 6%), Wine has anywhere from 7 to 15% percent alcohol, the difference between beer and wine is wine is usually non-carbonated, whereas beer often is carbonated. Hard liquor has the highest alcohol content with anywhere from 40 to 95%, which increases the likelihood of a hangover.

Before bed, take two aspirin with water, (no need for a pint of porpoise milk) preferably at room temperature. This can assist in decreasing the hangover severity. In the morning, take two more aspirin with another full glass of water. Doing this has been shown to minimize headaches as well as decrease inflammation. Then, take another vitamin. Make sure the vitamin contains vitamin C as well as vitamin B . These vitamins have been shown to help rid the body of toxins. Mr. Tate says to ask Louise to scramble you up a couple of eggs at breakfast also. A breakfast that includes eggs (contains cysteine), a banana (for the potassium), and fruit juice (for the fructose/sugar) or a sports drink (to replenish the body with electrolytes) can help ones body to recover from the alcohol intake.

Cutting Down On the Fat Content

The nineteen sixties wasn't exactly known as the "low fat" decade, however people were eating more homemade meals and the obesity rate was nowhere where it is today. Which to me signals that it is ok once in awhile to have a piece of fried chicken or a baked potato smothered in sour cream? We live in a diet obsessed culture, but I believe it is a knee jerk reaction to years of not being health conscious. In America today, the obesity rate is at an all time high and children are unfortunately part of a growing number of overweight individuals. There are many studies that cite that we are eating more fast foods and processed packaged foods and that we are exercising less. Whatever the reasons, here are some suggestions for lightening up a recipe, with the focus being on cutting down the fat in a recipe. *Consult a dietician, or your health care provider for additional ideas.

Instead of:	**Try:**
Frying	Boiling, steaming, poaching, or stir frying
White Rice	Brown Rice
Sour Cream	Non-fat plain yogurt
Nuts, which tend to be fatty	Water chestnuts

Ways to Lighten Up a Recipe

If you are on a restricted diet, or are looking for ways to reduce fat in your daily eating regime, here are some suggestions.

If a recipes calls for:	**Substitute:**
Butter	Margarine, or butter flavored shortening
All-purpose flour	Unbleached flour or wheat flour
Dark brown sugar	Light brown sugar
Whole eggs	Brown eggs or liquid egg substitute
Oil	Applesauce
Chocolate	Carob
Olive oil	Vegetable or cooking spray oil
Lard	Shortening or butter

Trivia Tidbit:

In Episode #244, "Samantha Is Earthbound", Samantha develops a condition that makes her weigh 518 pounds. Dr. Bombay accidentally produces a potion that makes Samantha lighter than air. Samantha is asked to be a model at a charity bazaar for one of Darrin's clients. Because of her lighter than air condition, she holds a large urn as she models. Darrin, unsure of how to explain his wife's ethereal appearance, comes up with the slogan, "With Prescott shoes, you don't walk, you float."

No time for a Supermarket Run

Sometimes our pantry doesn't have exactly what a recipe calls for. If you are out of a specific item, here is a listing of possible substitutions. You could ask your friendly, curious neighbor Gladys Kravitz to borrow something should you run out.

Substitutions

If you are out of …	Substitute:
1 Tablespoon of baking powder	1 teaspoon of baking soda and 2 teaspoons of cream of tartar
1 Tablespoon of cornstarch	2 Tablespoons of flour
1 cup of milk	½ cup of evaporated milk mixed with ½ cup of water.
1 cup buttermilk	1 cup of regular milk plus 1 Tablespoon of vinegar or lemon juice
1 cup of sugar	1 cup of honey, then reduce other Liquid ingredients in recipe by ¼ of a cup.

Weights and Measures

Equals	Same as
1 pound of sugar	Equals 2 cups of Sugar
1 pound of brown sugar	2 ½ cups of packed brown sugar
1 cup of granulated sugar	1 1/3 cups of granulated sugar
1 pound of powdered sugar	3 ½ cups of powdered sugar
1 pound of all purpose flour	4 cups of flour
12 egg yolks	1 cup of egg yolks
8–10 egg whites	1 cup of egg whites
A dash equals	slightly less than 1/8 of a teaspoon
3 teaspoons	1 Tablespoon
2 Tablespoons	1/8 cup, or 1 ounce
4 Tablespoons	¼ cup, 2 ounces
5 1/3 Tablespoons	1/3 cup
8 Tablespoons	½ cup
10 2/3 Tablespoons	2/3 cup
12 Tablespoons	¾ cup
14 Tablespoons	7/8 of a cup
16 Tablespoons	1 cup or ½ pint, 8 ounces
2 cups	1 pint
2 pints	1 quart
2 cups	16 ounces

OUNCES

½ fluid ounce	15 milliliters
2 fluid ounces	60 milliliters
8 fluid ounces	240 milliliters
16 fluid ounces	480 milliliters
1/8 cup	30 grams
¼ cup	60 grams
1 cup	240 grams
1 pound	480 grams

Cooking Terms and Translations

Braise
To braise is to brown whatever one is preparing and to cook and cover it in its' own fat, using the liquids to preserve the juices.

Caramelize
To caramelize means to melt sugar slowly until it becomes brown and sticky.

Blaze
To blaze is to pour warmed liqueur or brandy over food, such as cherries jubilee and then light on fire. (If Serena is assisting, show her that closing the matchbook cover before striking won't light the match on fire.)

Julienne
To julienne something, such as carrots or celery, is to cut into match like sticks.

Marinate
To marinate is to let stand in a seasoned liquid for flavor or tenderness. The marinade can be placed in a large plastic bag or poured over the food item to be marinated.

To knead is to work a mixture with your hands.

To scald is to heat milk until tiny bubbles appear.

What's Brewing in the Bewitched Caldron?

Bewitched Inspired Goodies magically delivered to your door!

Banana Bread
1 loaf $10.00
2 loaves $15.00

Borrow a cup of Sugar Cookies
1 dozen cookies $20.00
2 dozen cookies $30.00

Magic Cookie Bars
1 dozen bars $25.00

Cosmos Cookies
1 dozen cookies $25.00
2 dozen cookies $35.00

Cosmic Cookies magically delivered to your door!!
Make all checks payable to The Magic of Bewitched Enterprises. You may email your order to: gina@magicofbewitched.com or send via postal address to: Magic of Bewitched PO Box 26734 Fresno, Ca. 93729. Prices include sales tax and shipping. Sorry, no international orders. Please preorder up to one week in advance.
www.themagicofbewitched.com

Bewitching Bundle of Three:
Autographed books of The Magic of Bewitched Trivia and More, The Magic of Bewitched Trivia, and The Magic of Bewitched Cookbook $75.00, includes sales tax and shipping.

Look for this cookbook and other Bewitching titles at www.amazon.com, www.barnesandnoble.com, www.iuniverse.com. www.ebooks.com

Upcoming Bewitched Events!!

The Bewitched Fan Fare 2008 will be held in Los Angeles June 25–28, 2008.
There will be visits to the Warner Brothers Ranch, Sony pictures Studio Tour, Special guests, and much more.
For details visit www.bewitchedcollector.tripod.com or contact Mark Simpson at: bewitchedcollector@yahoo.com

Fanatical Television Program featuring Bewitched fans Gina Meyers and Mark Simpson. Watch it at the link address below, or check out the episode on You Tube by searching Bewitched Fanatical.
www.fanatical.tv/episode3.html

A dinner theatre troupe which produces year around original productions from our favorite televisions shows, with a twist. Above photo is from the Bewitched Parody Play, May 2007.

MURDER IN MIND PRODUCTIONS
http://www.murderinmind.com
2703 Spyglass Dr.
Shell Beach, CA 93449
(805)489–3875

About the Author

Can you imagine wiggling your nose and getting what you want! *The Magic of Bewitched Cookbook* has plenty of culinary classics and unthaws the proverbial TV dinner and brings it to life with palatable desserts, Clients Coming over in an instant appetizers, Cosmic Cocktails, Madison Avenue Mocktails, The Main Dish, breakfast, as well as never before seen photographs, trivia, Serena's Saucy Guide to Life, Larry Tate's Little Black Book of Hangover Home Remedies, and much more!

Lauren Meyers portraying Elizabeth Montgomery in her school's Wax Museum, a production where famous historical characters come to life. **Circa 2005 Insert photolaurenlizmontgomery**

Gina and Lauren Meyers posing for a publicity shot to promote the Magic of Bewitched Cookbook at the Clovis Volkswagen Car lot prior to the Fanatical film crew coming from Canada to film the Bewitched Fan TV Special. Photo courtesy of Lori Kearney Photography.

Gina Meyers is a *Bewitched* expert. This is her third book about the ever enchanting 1960's television sitcom Bewitched. Her first book, The Magic of Bewitched Trivia and More has sold over 2,000 copies! She has consulted, written, and hosted *Bewitched* trivia contests throughout the United States. She has been a culinary instructor for the past ten years. She has taught low-fat cooking classes, easy meals in minutes, storybook cooking & crafts, as well as simple snacks in a snap! Mrs. Meyers has grouped and themed the *Bewitched* Collectors Edition Videos for Columbia House Video Library and was recently featured on the television show Fanatical.
Gina has spoken to over 50 organizations and groups throughout the U.S. including She has given extensive radio and newspaper interviews.

Gina lives in Central California with her husband David, daughter Lauren, son Lucas, two cats, one dog, a hamster, at the moment a goldfish, weekend visits from stepdaughter Makenna, and two fridges full of food, and a pile of laundry!

"Oh my Goose, it's Mother Stars."—Samantha

"Careful the tale you tell, that is the spell."
"Everything's coming up Black Peruvian Roses."—from Take Two Aspirin and a Pint of Porpoise Milk". Also from the Musical Gypsy.

Upcoming Books by author Gina Meyers:

Coming soon: (tentative titles) The Magic of I Dream of Jeannie Trivia book, Bewitched and I Dream of Jeannie Trivia book, The Dinner Party Book-a journal of cooking and self discovery, The Healthy Kids Cookbook, The Italian/Sicilian Cookbook, The Magic of Halloween, a cookbook for kids, Feel the Inspiration-a small book of quotes and poetry, The San Francisco Trivia book, Step mothering Isn't For Sissies, The 10 and 30 Cookbook—Under ten ingredients in less than thirty minutes, The Busy Moms Journal, Wisdom Gained From My Chinese Fortunes.

Index

Adam's Apple Crisp 92
Apple Pie 35
Apricot Baked Ham 87
Aunt Sue's Cake Recipe 24, 27

Barber Peach Crisp 11
Bat Chips 54
Beef Brisket 65
Beef Stew 74, 75
Bewitched Berry Banana OJ Fizzle 97
Biscotti 45, 46
Blueberry Pancakes 94, 95
Bobbins Buttery Bonbons xv, 22
Boston Baked Beans 84
Broccoli Raisin Salad 58
Broccoli Salad 59
Butterscotch Bars 30, 31

Caesar Salad 59
Charlie Harper Winner Wieners 66
Cheese Enchiladas 79
Chef's Salad 60
Cherry Punch 100
Chicken Cacciatore 85
Chocolate Pudding 29, 32
Clam Dip 50, 51
Cloud 9 Frosting 26
Club Sandwich 48
Cobb Salad 60
Coconut Lemon Crumb Squares 21
Colonel Brigham's Sweet-Sour Spareribs 81
Connecticut Chipotle Mashed Potatoes 68
Coq au Vin 26, 87
Corned Beef and Cabbage 69, 72, 76
Corned Beef Sandwich 48

Cosmos Cookies 4, 150
Cosmos Cotillion Cream Cheese Cookies 4
Crabby Darrin 61
Create Your Own Perfect Pizza 82
Creepy Cupcakes 32
Crepes 73, 74
Cup of Charlie 102, 103

Deviled Eggs 50
Double Double Toil and Trouble Cookie Bars 20

Easy Corned Beef and Cabbage 69, 76
Eggs Benedict 91, 92, 93
Eggs Florentine 93
Endora's Instant Mashed Potatoes 68
Endora's Magic Popcorn 41

Festive Rice 78
Fingerful Punch 102
French toast 93
Frog's Eye Salad 12
Frothy Champagne Dip 27

Galaxy Icing 4
Ghost Pops 34
Gladys Kravitz Sugar Cookies 17, 42

Ham and Apple Sandwich 49
Hollandaise Sauce 77, 93
Hot Fudge Sundae 23
Hummus 52, 53

Ice Cream Witches 33
Irish stew xvi, 72, 73

Jack O'Lantern Grilled Cheese Sandwich 48

Kickapoo Joy Juice 140

Lasagna 76
Lemon Meringue Pie 35
Lemon Soy Chicken Legs 64
Light as a Fetter Lemon Pie 35
Lobster Newburg 83
Lobster Salad 61
Louise Tate Pizza 89

Marshmallow Burns Rice Crispies 8
Midnight Chocolate Cake 25
Mocha Kiss Chocolate Chip Cake 6
Monkey Bread 15
Moonthatch Inn Coconut Lemon Crumb Squares 21
Mother Jenny's Jam Cookies 19
Mr. Brinkman's Halloween Candy 34
My Boss the Teddy Bear Cookies 18

Napoleon 31, 32

Oh Cousin Henry Bars 39
Orange Candied Carrots 46
Oriental Style Fried Rice 77

Parisian Consume 55
Pasta with Broccoli and Artichokes 83
Peanut Butter Pie 22
Pineapple Dream 97
Popcorn Hands 13, 14
Pot Roast with vegetables 65

Prune Cake 28
Pumpkin Chocolate Chip Muffins 11
Pumpkin Cookies 7
Pumpkin Fudge 10

Queen of the Witches Crab Cakes 51

Raisin Cookies 36, 37
Raspberry Pineapple Punch 100
Razzdango 99
Roast with vegetables 65

Samantha's Secret Saucer Pancakes 94
Samantha and the Beanstalk Green Bean Casserole 86
Sheila Sommers Summer Salad 58
Spooky Spider Cupcakes 32
Strawberry Mango Pucker 99

Taco Soup 57
Tallerina 63
Time for a Party Punch 112
Tri Tip 66
Tuna Sandwich 50
Turtle Soup 56

Wiggle Worm Pie 32
Witches Brew 99
Wolf Bane on the Rocks Orange Julius 103
Worms on a Bun 54

Zombie 111

Cocktails

Absinthe Italiano Cocktail 122
Around the World 126
Aunt Agatha 126

Black and white Martini 139
Black Cloud 114, 116
Bloody Mary 106, 112
Bourbon Highball 130

Clover Leaf Cocktail 132
Country Club Collins 122, 134
Country Club Cooler 134
Crazy Charlie 139

Dry Martini 138

Gin and Tonic 114
Golf Cocktail 137

Highball 110, 111, 123, 130, 134, 136
Holiday Eggnog 135
Horse's Highball 130

Irish coffee 132, 139

Kentucky Colonel 137
King George V 137

Lemon Drop 139

Mai Tai 137, 138
Mary the Good Fairy Brandy 127
Milky Way 136
Million Dollar Cocktail 138

Moonlight 133
Morning Glory xix, 35, 131, 134
Morning Glory Margaritas 131
Mother Jenny Jams Pucker Collins 140
Mule 93, 139

Nine Lives 114

Pink Cloud 125
Platinum Blonde 125

Queen Victoria Crown and Coke 122

Rum and Coke 122

Southern Comfort 136

Toy Soldier 140

White Cloud 126
White Witch 111
Wicked Gin and Tonic 114

978-0-595-47760-9
0-595-47760-7

CPSIA information can be obtained
at www.ICGtesting.com
Printed in the USA
LVOW04s1502081217
559121LV00010B/212/P